Electric Liturgy

Dennis C. Benson

Unless otherwise indicated, Scripture quotations are taken from the
Revised Standard Version of the Bible, copyrighted 1946 and 1952.

Library of Congress Cataloging in Publication Data
Benson, Dennis C
    Electric liturgy.
    Accompanied by 2 phonodiscs (4 s. 8 in. 33 1/3 rpm.)
    1. Public worship. I. Title.
BV15.B44   264   72-175179
ISBN 0-8042-1593-6

© Dennis C. Benson 1972
Printed in the United States of America

 JOHN KNOX PRESS
Richmond, Virginia

Everyone is doing a book on liturgy. Good! Membership on a worship committee for a denomination or running several slide projectors during a contemporary liturgy seems to qualify one for the task. Perhaps anyone who has ever worshiped God should share his insights, complaints, and options.

I undertake this journey into the world of liturgy and celebration with you because so many people and their experiences are jammed into my head and guts. Hundreds of brothers and sisters have shared their risks in reaching out to worship God in fresh ways. These gifts and treasures given so lovingly belong out there with you. This print and sound experience is a naked lunch packed in the hope that it will refresh you as you do the truth of celebration as you can best do it with your folk. Many questions are raised in my mind by this quest. I hope that enough probes will spill out to provide a context in which you may charter a provisional direction for your own answers.

Let your mind and spirit wander into these print-electric lines and grooves. Many of the probes will become more fully developed by your head. Good! You might suspect that the quest I am undertaking is really my own search for a quality of life. It is. Perhaps that is also what celebration of worship is really all about.

Will the real Andy Warhol please stand up?

May 22, 1971—Carl just called. He wants me to lead a "far-out" worship service at the end of the summer. He is acting for a pastoral committee which supplies the University chapel during this period of time. My initial response is not too favorable. It sounds phony to have a different "freaky service" every week. Seems to make worship a show thing. However, I will do it. I am going to do it because I need to get up against the wall on this whole worship thing.

How can a person objectively sort out the process of worshiping God? What do you say when a person asks if you liked the service or not? This is a bit like asking a man married for fifteen years whether the state of marriage is good or not. It depends.

One religious person will say that he believes in the Word of God being preached. For him all other considerations are unimportant. The people's role is really secondary in his value system. Other brothers and sisters will stress the "individual" aspect of worship with others. On the other hand, some will evaluate the worship experience solely on the basis of how well the whole people communed with each other and with God.

There is an active block of worshipers who find "experimentation" in worship the key factor in labeling liturgy authentic. The jazz-pop-rock-dance-multimedia-sensual-visual service is the thing for them. However, what kind of worship to God is authentic? It appears that we are actually projecting our needs into the answer to that question. We tend to like and defend what meets our life demands and experience. This is why it is important that those working with liturgy struggle to know the baggage carried from the past.

**My life was
burning up.**

Well, it is easy for me to know the baggage I am carrying into the challenge offered to me by my friend. It has been five working days since I quit my job. It was a good job. I worked with good people. I have just left it all. I know there is no going back as far as my career is concerned. The job enabled me to grow as a person. The quality of my life, however, was tacky. How do you measure the celebration quality of life anyway? I guess that you know something is wrong when you feel the pinch. The wrinkles in my life finally rubbed my senses tender and I knew that something was wrong.

The two students enter my office for an orientation to mass media. They are only a drop in the endless stream of people who have made such stops during the past four years. They explain that they are just starting to do media for the University and City Ministries. Without a moment's break, I launch into the verbal and emotional barrage. The words and electric energy of the media madman within me pump out the content. Finally overload sets in upon the two fresh bodies. When they are overwhelmed, I fill their arms with print reinforcement to the emotional overload. Jim later tells me what I should have—would have known at a time when I was a more sensitive person: "You really turned them off. They felt that you didn't treat them as persons!" Nothing hits me harder than this kind of truth about myself.

Amy helps — do I help her?

Sunday night and it is already 7:00 P.M.! I have to get to KQV (ABC radio in Pittsburgh). It is time for weekly "Rap Around." Amy asks where I am going. "I am going to help people on the radio."
"Could I go and see the 'Rap Around' kids sometime?"
"No, there's no one at the studio. They call me on the phone."
"Could I help you do it?" I get the last of the eighty-five letters answered on cassette for later transcription by secretaries at the station. Five-year-old Amy comes into the study with several pieces of paper. She has written random letters of the alphabet on them. "Here are answers for the kids' problems." Wow! She is trying with every bit of her limited life experience to enter into my distant world. How have I crawled into her world lately?

The electric environment plays for keeps. I know what Felix felt when he threw the typewriter into the Central Park pond and shouted, "The bastard almost killed me!" The "owl and the pussycat" have to start all over again. They must discover what celebration and authenticity really mean. How did I get so screwed up in the electric environment? "How did a nice guy like you end up in a place like this?" I should have known that something was happening to me. It just kept growing and growing—more demands to do more and more.

"speeding" on media

A time arrived when I was working two or three nights a week—all night—in the audio studio. About three or four in the morning, my head would start "speeding." Fear would flood through my senses. I would lock all the doors on the floor. Noises haunted me with visions of strange attackers. Then I would start having "flashes." Even when I closed my eyes, the light kept streaming into my brain. All of this was from just an electric high—no chemicals.

There is something so compulsive about the electric nerve system which plugs into our brain and heart! I just couldn't resist it. It became an obsession. The next day at the office would be murder. I was not tired. The high would hang in there for days. After a week or so of this kind of agenda, I would come down—a real bummer. The downer would make me especially uptight with my love folk.

When you become electrified in our age, people ride on you. They are almost compelled to suck the highs from you. It is easier and safer than being a "conductor" for this electric energy themselves. The cheap thrills of another's high have always delighted spectator man. John Lennon's bitter outcry about the superstar's pain is clear. People mercilessly riding on the performer's musical extension of personal suffering is a point I understand. What makes me so mad in retrospect is that I loved to have people nurse on my electric juice! I begged them to keep sapping the energy I was wired to conduct.

It is ironic that the traditionalist or conservative really thrives on people who are enthusiastic or "spirit filled." The sad dilemma of this situation for many electric religious leaders and traditional people is that they are attracted to each other by the sugarcoating of excitement and support. Later they find that it is hard to swallow the whole pill. "Be filled with your message, but don't get us involved in housing for the poor, the feminist movement, or the other sources for your high."

"Support me and appreciate me, but don't question why I am high."

Of course, I cannot really divide my life into such clear highs and lows. I am dying and being reborn at the same time all the time. I am being electrically burned out and spiritually freed to celebrate new life at the same moment.

Being in the electric generator of media has changed my whole life. I can never shake what it has done to me. I hope not. The intersection of linear and electric existence is where the future is being won or lost. I am coming home to get it together in order to do that which I am called to do. What is this? Time will tell.

As I confront the possibility of constructing one worship service, everything that has ever happened to me comes flashing into my head. The electric age has filled me with PEOPLE. That's right. The technological-electronic environment has impressed upon my spirit the imprint of humanity! Thousands of letters, tapes, conversations, and body language experiences have blown my mind. The ideas and never ending stream of people people

they were hitchhiking on my head— and I loved it!

5

are now my present and future. The word "community" seems too shopworn to give expression to what I feel and know. There is no creativity outside of supportive relationships (actualized or otherwise). As a theological animal, I attribute this sense of flowing into humanity and personhood to the work of the Holy Spirit. The occasion of the Holy Spirit is community. Community is celebrated by people. Creativity is community. Electric media teases the participant by arousing his need for community without giving it or the capacity for him to create it. Modern man aches for fulfillment of this communal lust. The shape of the present family just can't provide the kind of support system being created and massaged by the electric environment.

*crunch—
deadlines—
dead-lines!*

Davis Yeuell called yesterday. The Book Editor of the John Knox Press wants to be assured that I will have the book and records for *Electric Liturgy* in Richmond on time. I assured him that all is well. However, it really isn't in good shape. This kind of reaction is part of my hangup from the days in the electric environment. How does a person with a Puritan work ethic make it in the overload arena? He kills himself! I will make my deadlines because my faith and upbringing command me to do it. The crunch between the past and present mind-sets is felt by all of us. How will these fifteen days of work before the deadline leave any time for celebration with my loved ones: Marilyn, Amy, and Jill? It will leave them no time at all!

The biblical accounts of man's encounters with God suggest that man learns about himself as well as his God from this experience. Moses resists the command and calling of God discovered through the medium of the burning bush. God knows Moses. He knows that Moses will understand himself only when he goes into Egypt to deliver his people. Paul, Peter, and a host of other saints weren't quite sure who they were until the self-knowledge revealed itself in their sense of calling. There is a sense of nakedness in the act of worship. It is a bit like making love. A person just can't hold back a part of himself or herself in such an encounter where there must be open giving and surrender.

What makes the process of worshiping and celebrating life so hard is that we don't always like what we find out about ourselves. We don't want to admit or share the reasons why meaningless symbols are important (or unimportant) to us. We may not want to manifest that which we hide from

God makes me face all of me — some isn't very nice

the world. Our baggage from the past may be overriding the very things God commands us to do and be. The interfacing of the nature of our God and our collective being is the basis of worship. Andy Warhol put on the art world recently when he sent out a friend to cover his campus speaking engagements. The schools thought that it was Warhol who was the speaker. Who is the real Andy Warhol? Maybe it makes no difference at all. However, in worship it is imperative that the person coming to celebrate brings himself completely. God calls for all of us. He wants us with hangups and all. He invites us to see him face to face. The age has set a number of stumbling blocks in the way of our confrontation. We are trained and rewarded for deception. It is cool for all age groups to be acceptably bland. "Don't dump your baggage (garbage) on my mind and heart. I have my own problems." Electric media takes me on fantasy trips. I can watch the suffering of other families and marriages in the afternoon TV programming. Saturdays and Sundays I can let other people beat out my hostility through the competitive games. At anytime I can plug into a headset and place somebody's song of joy, suffering, or anger in my head. Commercials provide the glue for my fragmented world. They string together that which doesn't fit together. Will the real me please stand up? I start my worship probe with this question.

Should I put a penny behind the fuse?

The liturgical systems are heavily loaded. In most settings the results are close to a "brown out" or a real "black out." People in charge of worship know that something is wrong. A lot of bailing wire and chewing gum is being used to meet the crisis. A penny may keep the lights on for awhile. However, "there is trouble in Center City." What is the nature of the liturgical crisis?

Nostalgia isn't history

History is the key to freedom. It shouldn't take George Orwell's probing to bring this point home to us. Just look around. The young like to create new forms without getting a reading on the situation from the past. Nothing happened before yesterday in the minds of some. However, even the mature have lost a sense of living history. The past is no longer that which can influence the present for many traditionalists!

The defender of the expected worship order or liturgy may deny this. He might assert that singing Gospel hymns, sayings beads, or reading the prayers of the fathers are meaningful and important because of history. This is not completely so. These manifestations of worship are important to such a believer. However, whether the original essence of these expressions is living symbols of the content is questionable. "History" in the mind of the worshiper usually means nostalgia. Today, I think that most people are coming to worship for this comfort factor.

A man in the audience of a multimedia show conducted at the University of Notre Dame spoke of this. After being confronted by five hundred slides projected on four screens, he claimed that he watched the one slide that was out of focus. "I couldn't make any sense out of it. However, it didn't move. Therefore, I kept watching it throughout the whole show." The whole world is moving and shifting. Mass media don't permit us the deception that things are the way they used to be. Everything is in constant flux. Only in liturgy can one experience the static. However, such freedom from change doesn't promise a truly historical perspective. Most often the traditional worshiper is grasping at a form of worship that goes back only fifty or a hundred years. Even the roots of this limited history are lost. The original meanings are often totally lost. There is no way to go back. It doesn't help to find the source of the common practices upon which so many liturgical forms are judged by weekly worshipers. A ritual or symbol once dead cannot be authentically revived as it was.

They/we want and need comfort and peace. There is something reassuring about seeing forms that do not change. Such comments can be made about "free" and "high" liturgical churches. Just try to change any worship aspect in a "free" church. The United Presbyterian Church experienced major hostility from members when it was suggested that the offering be moved from the position before the sermon to a location after the sermon. When a new directory for worship recommended that the sacrament of the Lord's Supper be celebrated each worship opportunity (instead of quarterly as is the case in the American Presbyterian tradition), the local churches just couldn't change. This had been true even when a major founding theologian, John Calvin, suggested the same practice. The local custom overrides a broader sense of history.

If people do embrace worship forms for reasons of comfort, it can be easily understood how so much anger is generated by the experimental "youth services" and "folk masses" that are being tried across the country. People come to gain assurance through familiar worship patterns and find guitars instead. Such a critique also tends to explain why preachers of Amos' or Micah's stripe get such anger from the congregation. The prophetic bite can easily short-circuit the comfort factor. Ted Gill has suggested that the church used to be a rescue mission, but now it is a comfort station. The Judeo-Christian tradition does offer comfort to those who are suffering and fearful. However, this limitation to the celebration of worship is a distortion. God demands as well as soothes.

Pop theology has replaced biblical faith

Another overload factor to existing liturgical expression is that it is built on a support system which no longer exists. For example, in the past the Protestant worship experience rested upon several other theological experiences. The faithful used to study the Scriptures (Sunday school) as part of the exercise of faith. Now only a very small number of church members do any kind of serious study of the faith. Most theology is learned through newsmagazines and article digests. Instant pop theology is the source of the Americans' faith.

Fellowship and mission were also inseparable parts of frontier-rural Protestant church life. These two factors are very weak in the life of most contemporary churches. Those who are involved in these aspects of the local congregation's work are often not participants in other theological functions. This means that in an earlier day the people of God brought a lot with them concerning the Christian faith to the worship experience. Forms of liturgy rested upon rich experience gained elsewhere.

The communication system of worship today is the same as in the past but without this kind of support structure. Liturgy is being overloaded when it has to deliver so many factors which are now missing. It just can't take it.

the worshipers related to Jesus, Moses, Joshua, and Paul —

but not to us!

Another difficulty besetting local celebrations of worship is that the feedback systems are inadequate. The worship leader no longer knows where the worshiper is in terms of needs, strengths, and interests. Co-worshipers do not know each other. A good example of this situation is the case of a pastor being concerned by reaction to his sermon. Two people call and say that somebody else is upset over what happened last Sunday. He panics with fear or anger (maybe both). He assumes that his job is on the line or that the whole congregation will be leaving. He has no feedback at all from the other three hundred people who were also present. What are they thinking and feeling? Why is Mr. Carlson looking out the window? Mrs. Sweeney is looking at the floor. What does it mean? What is going on here?

Religious people like to look upon their attendance at worship as an act of faithfulness. The meaninglessness of the experience almost makes it better from this perspective. You suffer boredom and thereby show your faithfulness. This seems to be a disappointing picture of God's nature. Did he create man for boredom or such meaningless "sacrifice"?

If it is conceded that the liturgical system is overloaded in a media sense, then what should we do? I do not have much sympathy for those who do their thing and the people "be damned." I remember spending an evening with a pastor who features dancing, drama, and other exciting art forms as part of worship. Marilyn asked about the congregation. He told my wife that it had been a congregation of about 150 people when he took over. She kept pushing. He finally admitted that there were only fifteen or twenty of the original people left. New people who liked these art forms had replaced those driven out by the experimentation. This kind of strategy raises some questions about ministry. What about those who are offended? Are we not responsible for the lost?

We are all programmed to a new time rhythm!

There are also a number of givens about most liturgical forms which make valid worship communication in the electric age difficult. The TV commercials have changed our attention span. After forty television spot advertisements, a thirty-minute block of input presented by one person with low dramatic drive is hard to follow. Most liturgy leaders give lip service to the corporate importance of public worship. Yet, most worship settings are impersonal and difficult. It is hard to commune with my brother when I only see the back of his head. It always seems that pews are hard and the legroom limited. It is also clear in most houses of worship that what is up front is the most important. Those who get control of the worship leadership are the focal point. No matter how much we speak to the contrary, the leader is the key factor.

As I sit and think about the Heinz Chapel event, I realize that something is happening to me as a person. The overload of the electric environment is slowly being suppressed by the need to celebrate and worship as a person. Amy and Jill help a lot. Amy is five and everything becomes a celebration for her. She wants to celebrate birthdays, a friend dropping by, a trip to be taken, even Misteroger's daily appearance! Jill is two. Her words are scrambled, but in more abundance every day. When she gets excited and appreciative about the joy of living, her arms pump up and down. She even jumps up and down when happiness possesses her!

We must unknowingly have talked a great deal about dreams. When Jill returns to us from her nap, Amy asks about her dreams. "Butterflies and puppies," she proudly shares with us. "Good butterflies and puppies or bad?" "Good butterflies and puppies."

Five-year-old Amy blows my mind when she gets word that something delightful is about to happen. A strange kind of spirit comes over her. She starts talking seriously concerning the procedures about to unfold. She becomes possessed with the breaking forth of good things. My daughter is transported to a reality which transcends other realities.

Amy and I have a day of celebration!

Today is particularly good. Amy and I have a day together—five wonderful hours of celebration. We walk in Point State Park. We trace where the three rivers come together. Amy spots the pollution in the water and delivers her lecture on spoiling nature. We stretch out on the unbelievably green grass, I on my back with Amy's head on my stomach. A couple to our left passionately kiss and roll on the lawn. It's that time of year. Five happy members of a family eagerly unpack a lunch on our right. A sixth member sits apart from the circle and pouts. We stroll among the freaks, retired men, cops, and Jesus people. Amy asks for a penny. She makes a secret wish and drops the coin into the dirty water of the Allegheny. We walk hand in hand in the sparkling day. She moves along with jumping steps which push me to take bigger strides. She is joy, love, and happiness. It is a special day of celebration for us.

A lot is happening to me during these six days without work or a regular paycheck. Marilyn is fresh and exciting. It is good to know her again. It is a bittersweet joy to discover how we have grown and changed these past few years in separate worlds. We had been ruined by those first five years of totally intermixed lives. We must again allow our lives to merge.

It is a new and yet familiar joy to cuddle close to her in the night. What joy and delight there is in the body and spirit of the one you love. The wonder of love makes you want to cry, but you laugh uncontrollably instead. What celebration in the arms of love! How can you say what you feel when your whole being is filled with love? Yet, these moments of joy will undoubtedly be blurred by the rubs of encounter which must make up a daily relationship. It is hard coming down after being close to "black out."

These past few days have allowed my mind to clear and become even more intermixed with experience than before! So many things flood into my mind. I just can't slow it down. Every moment of experience from the past stays with me and gives meaning to the newest moment of existence. Objects, persons, and ideas keep merging to form new creations. The possibilities of creating the new from the old seem so endless.

A tape came today from Jane Mall. This creative teacher shares and now I hear completely. She touches my spirit and her voice sinks into me. Her capacity to ride on the gifts of her students is too much! The love of her brothers and sisters near and far reaches out and embraces me. I play her tape over and over again. The volume and change of her voice tone allow me to get into her head and mind.

It's too much!

Where does all of this end and where does it begin? How do I keep my madness from the electric age and how do I securely anchor my celebration of God? Does a person ever untangle all these threads? How can the overloaded traditional liturgical system be appealing even after such a day of celebration with Amy?

I suspect that these questions are the focal points of the quest for valid worship. We must mix the personal and corporate dimensions of worship in order to find a style of celebration fitting our personhood. This may be the only way out of the overload and senility in so much contemporary worship experience.

Peanut Butter, but no jelly

Amy likes her favorite lunch fixed in a certain way—"peanut butter, but no jelly, Nestlé Quik with a straw." For a number of reasons there are many givens in each worship situation. The way-it-has-always-been-done mentality is an acute factor. People always use this as the basis of judgment. The mind-set takes on an almost divine sanction. Maybe this is just the way that God has meant for his people to meet him. Ironically, few people would ever admit this to be the case. It just seems right to have things the way they have been. A sad thing with this situation is that when the church wants to swing out and meet people where they are the process is just reversed. They throw everything away and look for tricks to win the "kids." Such a stance fools no one. The young people feel uncomfortable with this well-meaning, but aimless approach. Of course, many of the former worshipers are lost.

Perhaps it is wise to survey the givens in most worship communities. A building is part of the freight. Unfortunately, it is geared for the lecture hall mentality. The focus is on the speaker. Lip service is given about the "center of worship" and the like. However, we all know that the man who commands the space where all eyes must fall is the center. This given makes some other goals almost impossible to achieve (i.e. fellowship or transpersonal theological exchange among worshipers).

If the speaker is not the total center, he shares it with a choral group. The old Protestant frontier ideal of the whole people singing praises to God has been reduced to the "show and sing" philosophy. Churches are proud of their singers. The strong churches (large ones) most often will have paid

It's what's up front that counts!

13

people from outside the community to do the singing. In fact, the "ministers of music" often command large salaries and have a heavy influence on the content of the service. Why shouldn't they? If worship is a showcase to impress God, why not put the best up front?

There is also the inheritance of environment in most worship settings. My mother often talks about "church odor." She is talking about the way old hymnals and aged carpeting smell when the room is not often aired. Church basements have a character and environment that can never be forgotten. There are always walls painted some shade of green. The floors have imprinted shuffleboard games. Where else do you see painted basement walls? Most bellies of the worship center also contain old furniture. (Why throw anything away? Just give it to the church.) and under-used kitchens. These working areas of the religious institution have a set environment which is like no other in the society. Most local schools certainly don't have this kind of secondhand, yesteryear character. Few businessmen in the congregation would put up with this kind of equipment for their place of work. Rare is the family which can withstand the commercial picture of how their home should look and keep the castoffs it started out with.

Throughout the building of worship you usually see ancient bits of brass (in need of polishing) which claim "Dedicated to the Glory of God in loving memory of. . . ." The dedication and memory seem to have faded with the passing of time. The light within the worship environment is also a given. It usually comes streaming through pseudo-stained glass. The milky or tinted glass may sport pictures supposedly from the Bible. For the young the visual concept of God and his chosen ones is impressed upon the mind forever.

The print environment is presented as straight linear. The information about worship is "ordered." There is a beginning and an end. The substance cannot be missed or avoided by anyone. One can sleep through the experience and have it all in his pocket upon leaving. (Whatever happens to the bulletins taken home by people? Are they a kind of receipt for services rendered?)

I know. Such a picture is a straw church. No such religious animal is constructed just like this. However, there is enough of the familiar in this description to be unnerving. The sad thing about such givens is that when

Wander through your church building and view it through the eyes of a stranger or "It's all right for funerals — I would never want to live there"

the church does have a chance to change these factors through building or renovation nothing happens. The worship committee and controlling board just make it bigger, brighten the paneling, change the carpeting (not the color), and paint the walls. The choir is elevated a little higher. The organ is expanded. Such tinkering suggests that the wine may be getting the wineskin which fits. The content hasn't changed so why should the environment change? However, in the electric age the givens of this morning will not be the same this afternoon. Every person in the society is aware of this reality. He has emotional wounds to prove it.

Amy demands her peanut butter, but no jelly, regularly. However, she has no responsibility to it. It is there when she wants it. The church is trapped in this kind of situation. The members of a church or parish use the church as a worship center when convenient. However, few members will serve with the faithfulness they give to their lodge or service club. Members of those luncheon clubs will travel to another city in order to make up missed meetings. They will put up with ridicule and childish games in order to be faithful members. Young people and adults will memorize a fantastically complicated ritual for the lodge rites. However, these same people will go to worship when it is convenient. Most members barely know their worship service ritual. Even the clergy (particularly the Protestants who don't use the sacraments often) have to read the promise of the sacraments to their people!

Does God live in a tomb?

Another given that must be faced when one examines the foundation of modern worship celebration is that the religious institution deals with its income in a certain way. Most older religious facilities are under-used and over-serviced. In most cases more money is spent on the upkeep of the buildings than on the educational upkeep of the people. Yet, the religious structures aren't going to disappear tomorrow or the next day. They will be around in roughly (sorry for the choice of word) the same form we see them today. The people may be gone, but the stone and bricks will stand gloriously maintained in the future. Many buildings have been assured immortality through the generous gifts of the saints who have passed on. The ongoing support of the religious unit is usually concentrated in the heavy giving of a few families. It is amazing to examine the donation profiles of modern churches. A small percentage care and give a great deal. The rest ride along on minimum dues.

These nuts-and-bolts financial givens are important for one trying to get a reading on the environment in which worship is sought. That beautiful moment in the "Jesus spots" (produced by the United Methodist and United Presbyterian Churches) comes to mind. Actor Tim Hardy, who plays Jesus, reaches out and feels the rich young man's garment. He laughs gently, "You love it all, don't you?" Yes, we do!

guilty thoughts on a Sunday morning

I always feel guilty when this happens—I missed church again today. Yet, it is so hard when I do go. Is it just the lack of faithfulness that makes me so restless? I try to follow what is going on. For awhile I used to think that it was just professional sensitivity that encouraged me to find so much to be distracted by in the worship service. I now know that this isn't a good explanation. There is something wrong with the structured nature of the worship agenda as it meets my needs. It just doesn't have the vibes of the world that turns me on daily. Is it just being super-hip for a person to claim that he may feel more communion being actualized with friends at a pot party than in the average church with neighbors and fellow church members? It probably isn't true. However, I somehow resent that it is forced upon me. I get the feeling that they—the people around me—also are turned off. Why do so many of them go to sleep during the sermon? Why do so many just stand and look around when the congregation is supposed to be singing? Is it just the short fuse my attention span now has because of the "ten in a row" top forty station that makes me tune off after five or ten minutes?

My daughter is turned on by the church school. She likes to have me go. How long will it be before she will join me and other worshipers in this restlessness? How do we wear away the early enthusiasm that the children seem to have in the beginning?

I need to press the flesh!

Even when something does happen to me worshiping in this church, I leave with an uncomfortable feeling. It is as if I have been sexually teased, but there is no satisfaction. When the Word of God has hit me in the face, I need to do the truth with my brothers and sisters. However, they split so quickly. I am high and no one can bring me down. Pentecost has happened but there are no small groups in which to do the truth (e.g. Acts 2).

I am sitting in the church service and my mind keeps flashing somewhere else. I try to let my head run in the prayer groove being cut by the worship leader. However, my head wanders to other things. My mind does the kind

16

of thing it used to do when educational settings were unbearable. I kind of daydream about another time as another person.

It is quite frustrating to be there. I know that if I were in the place of those two worship leaders, it would be just as boring for this folk who have gathered to worship God. Is it bigger and more hopeless than we all realize, or is this what God demands? Am I free or do I want "peanut butter, but no jelly"?

I will have to deal with these questions now that I will bear the responsibility to enable worship to happen this summer. Will the folk in the University chapel be as restless as I am?

You can score even when you are short

Woody Allen knocks me out. He lets his inner frustrations hang out for us to understand through humor and pathos. He often fantasizes in his comedy routines about how a person might score with the opposite sex even when he is short. Woody is short. He knows that it can be hard in our society to make points with women with this socially unacceptable physical feature.

The pockets of renewers and innovators in most local settings keep coming back to liturgy and worship books with the response: "Yes all that is nice, but. . . ." They have been through the bloody battles to overcome the kind of analysis which we have thus far shared about the local or particular unit of religious faith. These caring folk have come out on the short end.

The youth service was fun to work on. The kids got a real kick out of spending weeks preparing it. However, they are still getting feedback from some of the regular worshipers. "It didn't seem like worship." "It wasn't dignified enough for true worship." "Weren't the kids cute!" "It was all right until they played all that loud noise."

As you may have gathered from this rambling reflection on worship, I have a particular approach to celebration. I am convinced that we must carefully make our way through a lot of underbrush to find the direction we are trying to pursue in local situations. This process of actualizing authentic celebration in the worship of God is risky. The undergrowth will be prickly and scratchy. There is always the possibility that the quest to confront God authentically as a people will be missed completely. It is easy to get lost on the way.

There are some indicators from those who have been creatively at the task for some time. How can you do the truth truthfully and yet accomplish all the goals embedded within the liturgical experience? The answers we find for a particular worship experience at Heinz Chapel will be the answer. The full answer to these questions can only be found in local worship. This is the focus of authentic provisional answers to most theological crises. All of us speaking to broad audiences must in the final analysis give way to that local group of brothers and sisters. They are the focus of the Holy Spirit. It is there that the Holy Spirit will enable the Word to become flesh and dwell among them. This happens because and in spite of them.

When I am enabling worship in a local situation I use one approach. My favorite strategy on scoring locally in fulfilling the quest for celebration grows out of this prejudice for local folk. There are a couple of options for the restless people who want more complete worship. They can attack the trouble through confrontation. This means that the youth service or other special opportunity becomes the beachhead. Give it your all when the stage is yours. It does make you feel a certain satisfaction. However, this approach has certain risks. You are likely to feel the backlash of those who have had their nostalgia needs disturbed. They will dump their emotional acting-out of discomfort (anger, disappointment, or sorrow) on the folk who gave you a chance. That great pastor or rabbi will get it in the neck for giving you the chance. There will also be a huge coming down for you when it is over. You will have worked so long for this fresh worship experience. Where do you go from here? How do you get the shaving cream back into the aerosol can? Another thing that bothers me about these showcase experiences is that they take on an "entertainment" character. The open celebration of community with God and your neighbor is more than an art form. It is that—and much more.

A second possibility is a quiet campaign with the committee or ruling group which shares worship responsibilities with the pastor. This can be done

Scheming for change!

through study documents carefully placed in the hands of those who make the decisions. It might even be possible to give some of these key people the experience of celebrating worship in another liturgical context. Take them to a church having such fresh worship opportunities. "Take an elder to a worship service of your choice this week." Some creative worship folk have combined this strategy with the first one. They do a creative celebration for their church. Then they gather support from a number of sources. Perhaps news of the service is shared in a newsletter like "Recycle" ("Finding new creative use for existing resources"). Two or three hundred letters may be received from people interested in what has happened in your church. You then let the boards and congregation know about the wide interest in this kind of celebration. The range of inquiries will indicate interest within all the major theological thrusts. Every part of the country will be represented. This makes the skeptic realize that your group is really in the mainstream of liturgical probing.

Support each other!

The drawback of this kind of approach to change in your context is pace. It will be very slow. Too much will ride with each experimental opportunity. Corporate worship should not be loaded with excess baggage. It should maintain a simplicity of purpose and thrust: the conformation between God and his collected people.

There is also the approach which demands absolute power. It does happen sometimes. The people in charge simply create the new liturgies they feel are valid. This does two things. It will attract people who don't attend now. It will also clear out many of those who find meaning in the older forms of celebration. This style of liturgical renewal raises questions which are hard to resolve. What do we owe the people caught in the crunch of change? How homogenous do we want a worshiping group to become in terms of values?

Folk! One way to develop fresh worship forms

The stance which seems to be most promising for those who are located in "ordinary" situations of faith is what can be called the "folk" approach. The term "folk" is used here as a collective term for brothers and sisters who have it "together." They share the capacity to feel each others' "vibes." In this strategy for rediscovery of worship, a small group of "folk" secures permission to experiment for a six-month period with an alternative worship experience. This move has the advantage of getting official status. The optional hour should be noncompetitive with the other services.

The length of time for the probes into celebration is quite important. The folk have to learn together who they are, what they are to celebrate, and how to bring it all together authentically. This style of discovery is really grounded in the history of the church.

Acts 2:37-42 gives us some clues about how some of the early fathers built a style of communicating as celebration. After the individual, separated people from everywhere were struck to the quick by the proclamation of Peter and the presence of the Holy Spirit, they went into small groups. In these contexts they celebrated life together: study, fellowship, worship, and the going forth to perform miracles.

The folk manner of worship will always have a small base at first. However, in several places where this style has been used things have changed in just a few months. One church had four hundred people attending the alternative worship experiences at 8:00 A.M. Sunday mornings.

It cannot be promised that things will always work out the way you want them to. One brother used this style of approach to liturgy only to find that the strong following threatened the senior pastor. It was one of the factors which led to his firing. Meaningful celebration of worship can be dangerous!

How do you measure what has happened in a worship experience? How do you know that you have scored? Most summers I do supply work. This means that I cover for vacationing pastors. I know that the liturgy should present a full picture of the Good News. The sermon is just part of the whole picture. However, that is not true in reality. I likened this kind of worship leadership to a strafing mission. We just drop a few bombs and blast the roads and byways—hoping to be on target. I hate such martial imagery. However, there is this kind of aggressiveness about the hit-and-run preacher. If they say they liked your sermon at the door after the service, should you be happy or insulted?

Last year just about this time of the year I participated in a series of unbelievable worship experiences. The celebrations were almost always part of an intense weekend or length of time in which some real struggle had been undertaken. We were into each other's hearts. At these times of being "folk" it seems that a communion with God is also easier. One crazy

there have been good times!

service lasted for two hours! We were totally unaware of the passage of time. We had planned it as a community. We knew that we had scored!

One summer Sunday I took the pulpit at a nearby church. It was a big church. I am not used to preaching before a lot of people. I would not have been invited if Dave, the assistant, hadn't strongly urged that I be the guest preacher. It just seems that a long-haired minister is not invited to preach in the churches of my denomination in our area. Other traditions are great about their hospitality. However, there is a bit of uneasiness among my brethren about their "far-out" colleague. This kind of mentality is usually the result of an overactive imagination. After the service one lady confessed that she had laughed when she saw "all that hair." "I am not laughing now," she said. The grasp of her hand was warm and loving.

They were afraid during that service!

I remember the crisis I created for the church folks who live in Waynesburg, Pennsylvania. I had been invited in April to preach at this church in June. It seemed quite natural. My wife was a member of the congregation and I was the chaplain at the college in the community. However, in early May I was fired. The reason for the dismissal was linked in most minds to my activity in organizing black and white students to stop housing discrimination in the community. The church fathers didn't know what to do. What would this outcast do in our pulpit? It was a strange experience. Did they think that I would use my responsibility as worship enabler to attack my enemies? Would I try to score at their expense? Their fear supports the kind of misunderstanding that is current among worshipers. Or is it that they have had such bad celebration experiences that such fears could be founded on what had happened before? Unless some enablers take a posture of community there will be no authentic "scoring" as people celebrating their God.

Play it again, Sam

One of the most embarrassing moments of my youth was the time in church when I was enthusiastically singing with a favorite girl friend. We had

I can't sing!

come to church together and I was anxious to impress her. Halfway through the hymn she noted that I was looking at the wrong page in the hymnal! The song had two tunes and I had chosen the wrong one. I guess that I have not tried to hide my lack of musical skills since then. My friends and family tell me that when I open my mouth, it is clear to the world that I have no musical talent. At what point in the worship of God should you share total lack of such talent? Is it better to keep quiet and not bother those who want to stay on key?

If I believed in reincarnation, I know what I would want to be the next time around. I would have to request new skills to fit my dream. I didn't get them this time out. I would like to be a musician. Probably someone within the whole pop-rock-folk mode would be my choice. I can fantasize about the freedom to be able to channel all my feelings and energy into something others can feel. It would probably be agonizing to know that even then others would not have the capacity to do something with the feelings being picked up.

It is funny how music takes on meaning and feeling once you get into it. After listening many times the sound gets into your head. I am now listening to Paul and Linda McCartney's *RAM* LP. The first time through it seemed confusing and bewildering to me. It now carries overtones missed on the first exposure.

Music also wears out with me. At least, there are times when I am just not into something like I was last time. Certain LP's are chosen for certain reasons, I guess.

The worship at my ordination has particular meaning for me. It seems that the choir and the people were so much a part of the musical extension of what was happening. Of course, I got to choose the hymns. Did the music really mean as much to others as it did to me? Could this music act as a means of the kind of experience needed to be authentic music for their worship? Does music carry you to an emotional-intellectual level of worship or do the thoughts and memories of the past which you bring with you make music meaningful?

A wedding ceremony unfolds. The people select music to express this important day. The people come to worship and participate in a great life ritual. Critics in the world, church (Vatican), and elsewhere claim that

Emotional music in worship

people on such occasions often choose tasteless music. It has neither art nor theology, claim many. Should it be better theology and art—or what is apparently meaningful to the people calling forth the occasion of the event?

Nineteen seventy-one was the year of *Jesus Christ Superstar.* The Webber-Rice composition was the pop favorite of those trying new things in church music. I must have seen reports from over a hundred churches which used it in some form or another. Yet, many people were concerned by the wide religious acceptance of the pop-rock religious musical. As expected, many of the faithful were offended by sounds which they assumed were not proper for inclusion in the worship experience.

Pop music

From what source should music for contemporary worship come? The music seems to flow from people people. The folk folk have always made music and love. The religious community has always tapped such environmental sources for the rhythm of its songs and prayers in praise of its God. Even the standard Protestant Gospel hymns have common roots. Some of the tunes come from the tavern or pub. There is even a story around about two professors who write contemporary Gospel hymns as a commercial lark. They deliberately write songs as spin-offs of pop tunes. They have found that they can get $500 to a $1,000 for these quickies. The lyrics do not reflect their outlook or faith. It is a religious Tin Pan Alley for them.

Strange things happen to music in the hands of a religious person. He is able to transform his vehicle of worship and sever it from the roots it had. The hymn becomes familiar and heavy with holy meanings. It becomes an end in itself.

It is even strange to think about the role of music in most worship services. Why is it used at all? For some the beauty of musical expression is a fitting gift to God. This kind of understanding has inspired great musicians to create musical treasures. However, this is not the kind of music which is requested by the faithful in most local settings.

Who really sings anymore?

Protestants and Vatican II Catholics may claim that music should be a means of corporate expression concerning praise and adoration in the presence of God. However, Protestants no longer sing. Just watch most congregations during the hymn time. Very few sing. I have elsewhere expressed concern over the role now being assumed by paid singers who do the work of singing the music for the congregation. Many of the older saints are just too tired to sing. Their lungs can no longer take the kind of work demanded by singing. One social commentator claims that a movement can be evaluated by the role of singing in it. He uses the example of the union movement. During the years of high participation and wide rank-and-file support, there was strong group singing. The singing has now waned. So, he claims, has the membership support of the movement. I hate to submit the religious institutions to such a judgment. Singing just may not be a valid means of corporate expression of feeling. Many people in our country today do not (or cannot) sing the National Anthem at baseball games!

It is confusing to look at the status of music in our culture. It is true that music as a source of expression for the common faith expression is very limited. However, at the same time, there is more interest in writing and playing pop music among young people than ever before. There are hundreds of rock combos in every major city. They spend hours practicing and trying to write music. The individual combo expresses its solidarity through music. The children of the electric age share community through the common celebration of music on LP's and radio. It is their tribal drum. Yet, they do not sing for institutions of faith (in the traditional sense). Maybe this is really a reflection of the status of modern man's relationship to institutional forms in general. However, I don't think music plays the same kind of role in faith communities as it used to.

copping pop
for Jesus

If these comments suggest a valid analysis of the situation, we must look at the use of music in worship very carefully. A lot of people are trying to do something with pop-rock-folk music in liturgy. There is a wealth of original church music being written by a number of people. On the other hand some local groups take pop songs and change the main words to give them a particularly religious meaning. John Ono Lennon's, "Give Peace a Chance" becomes "Give Christ a Chance." Most often this kind of folk likes to take love songs and change the girl to Jesus or God in the lyrics. This use of material seems a bit too contrived.

The pop-rock world has been into a Jesus-religious trip for the past couple of years. The top one hundred always have a number of religious-message songs. In recent years these religious tunes have won a big following.

Even the sound of the old Gospel hymns' sound draws the composer's attention (i.e. Simon and Garfunkel, country-western material, etc.). Many people were concerned when *Jesus Christ Superstar* hit the nation. "Were these men Christians?" This seems to be a strangely irrelevant question for our age. If the church depended on motivation for its literature, music, and customs from the past, there would be very few practices that would stand up.

Rock "masses" and liturgies have followed an earlier interest in the use of the jazz idiom. However, there have been few uses of these kinds of musical forms which have really incorporated the worshiping people of God. Most often such beautiful works of art are performed for entertainment. There is nothing wrong with theologically sound and artistically moving works of art. However, this is not often the kind of celebration which meets the needs of local people. They can't afford good art and have trouble grasping sound theological anchors when art is found.

Folk music

Folk music has been a favorite of most local religious units. There is something naturally religious about good folk forms. The "folk mass" has found popularity in a number of Catholic parishes. However, this does not seem to be enough change as far as the needs of the closed person is concerned when he faces worship. He is often asked to sing the songs and he is hesitant about making this idiom his faith expression.

The most interesting aspect of worship and music on the scene today is that of original works developed by local people. This kind of giving to celebration calls for special talent. However, such talent is more abundant today than at any other time. The pop combos practicing in garages in most urban complexes are rarely asked to share their talent with local religious institutions. Why not commission them to work with your worship committee on special music? They might be happy to exchange their gifts for a place to practice.

Mose Henry

Mose Henry is another creative music man of religious celebration. Mose and I stumbled upon each other by accident. I was rescued from an insular conference in Florida by two young pastors who wanted to show me where the action was really at. We pulled up to a Presbyterian church which embraced black and white members. A small building next to the church was the location of the coffee house. I was impressed by the hate and love wall. Painted in vivid colors it screamed out the crunch between two forces within the culture. I was more impressed, more imprinted by Mose. He willingly sang his own songs of love, life, and faith which flowed from his heart and guitar. The former lead singer for the Highwaymen explained that many of his friends in the music world fell back upon the acoustical guitar for composing. He liked the closeness of the instrument to his body. He could feel its rhythm and let it express the beat of his body and heart.

Mose and I have known each other in other contexts. I have seen him take a hymn like "Joy to the World," and turn a whole room of old ladies upside down. They actually took the favorite religious songs of the past and reshaped the same material into new forms. When the one hundred women hit "Joy" under Mose's encouragement, the hymn somehow seemed brand new, and yet ageless. Was he suggesting some basic direction in worship music by this fleshing out of meaningfulness and contemporary rhythm? Mose now travels the country helping people do their faith through music. "I am giving God the best that I am."

Myron Slater

Myron Slater is a pastor with ordinary-extraordinary talents in this direction. He has been setting sections of Kansas ablaze with his Old Testament translations. He has not been satisfied simply to translate the Hebrew into fresh English. He has set the biblical stories in the form of plays and musicals. Myron has tried to combine a couple of the options suggested here. He uses familiar hymn tunes as vehicles for his English translations of the biblical stories. Myron has done extensive work on the Psalms. He will probably be snapped up by a publisher and we will see his work as being "professional." However, it is important to remember that the source of this creative work of celebration has been the local Chanute, Kansas congregation.

A number of the brethren who work on liturgy have taken contemporary music and rewritten the lyrics. This first emerged in the camping circuit where folk songs suddenly started bearing new words. This has been effectively done by enabling groups of worship people in local settings when done carefully. Roger Boekenhauer has combined a Christian education function with a worship expression by having his junior highs take the tune from a pop favorite and write new lyrics to it. The thrust of the learning experience may be church history or the Bible. The students have an opportunity to restate what they are learning as a song and then use it in worship. Several of these have stayed with the group for the course of the church year. These songs have special meaning to those who created them. There is so much talent within our local setting! One of the greatest failures of contemporary religion is its ignorance concerning the gifts of people. The faith community simply has no index on the treasures its people can really bring in the worship of God.

Worship and trivia

So often people like to think of evangelism as part of worship. The area of music as an authentic expression of faith can be one of the most important dimensions of touching those who have shrunk from the faith. Ask a man to bring his art (expressed or appreciated) and he brings the channels where his faith can be expressed. In other words, we are suggesting that man's trivia is an important dimension of his existence. The garbage of his life is part of the man. Folk legend Bob Dylan continues to have devoted fans. Some people are cultists about him and his private life. One of these fans has spent the past five years collecting every bit of information concerning his hero. He recently reported a number of new Dylan stories. He said that he got this information through his systematic search of Dylan's daily garbage! If we really want to know with whom we are communicating, we must take his idle interests seriously. Ecologists are giving this position a twist and showing us how important garbage really is. Man may undo himself with what he throws away.

The role of music in worship must be probed by those seeking to enable authentic worship to take place. How does music fit into worship? Is it a set of wings which can enable the people to have a trip into deeper communication with the source of their existence? The danger with all music is that it may be a bridge from one part of the service to the next. This "filler" or "traveling music" function seems to have a very limited usage. Yet, I suspect that this is how music is utilized by most worshiping bodies.

Artist or critic

It might be interesting to explore with your people just what role singing plays in their lives. I would suspect that singing is no longer the corporate manifestation that it once was. Maybe in the world of heavy entertainment input the individual feels unable to be the performer. He either performs (like the many kids with their groups) or he is the audience for music. This shift should suggest many clues for the worshiping community. It means that your people may be highly sensitive to the quality of music. The old

27

complaint of performers may still hold true: "You are either creative (artist) or you are a critic." We have lots of critics. The critic or audience function may be very creative. However, it means that the traditional response of singing every hymn may not be the expression most fitting for this community of electric people. They don't want to sing when they know that their voices are not as good as those which they are accustomed to hearing on record or tape.

How does man musically express himself in the worship of God? The response to such a question must be probed on the local level. Have you ever been asked about how you feel about singing in a group of strangers? The solution of just having the choir do it does not seem the best. I am not against the talented people in the congregation doing their music as their gift to God. However, this does not solve the problem of finding a musical means by which every man has a chance to release all of himself before his God. At another time in history there used to be participatory musical services where the whole community just sang. These "hymn-sing" services are disappearing from the religious landscape. Urban-electric man simply doesn't feel that singing is an authentic means of self-expression. The preparation services of the past enabled the people to sing more comfortably in the regular worship setting. Whether there can or should be a revival of congregational singing is a good question. The electric age moves in a strange course. The bold and new cut up the meanings of the past effectively. There is still a role for history and tradition. However, when the past reemerges in this electric environment, it is different from the way it used to be. This is very important to the religious man. He has not always understood this. Faith has often bred the naïve hope of "reviving" things. Revival and resurrection are two different concepts. Revival suggests that you can pump more air ("wind" is what the church usually uses) into the slumbering body. Enough air and the giant will stir again. Once the form is inflated it will be the same as before. However, such a view also suggests that there was once a golden age. Faith memory easily degenerates into wishful thinking about things that never were. There really never was a perfect age of faith in the course of history.

On the other hand, resurrection suggests real death. It is over. It is finished. Yet, through some miracle a new life is created from the beauty of the older form. Perhaps we should keep the resurrection concept before us at

Revival or resurrection

all times when we probe forms of worship. Resurrection also permits us the freedom to see the cracks and scars on the "old man" or dead form. Resurrection can be a powerful concept in dealing with the past, present, and future. Music then is part of a complex puzzle. As we view each piece, we must also keep juggling these other lingering questions.

It can't be; he has yellow teeth

A lot of people hate the question "Who am I?" "I never asked that when I was a kid." Well, it is a hard question to deal with. It's a hostile question because we really don't know how to get a grip on it. Perhaps we should make that quest with a group as suggested in the past few pages. However, we must realize that the personal search for identity in structuring celebrations, is inseparable from our quest for a grasp on the reality of God. Most worshipers would list something having to do with God as a main reason for worship. However, beyond this general sense of Deity there is often a muddled understanding of the source of celebration.

worship as a reach for God

The enablers of worship and those doing worship as a people must struggle continually with the desire to know God. Somehow I don't think that we can ever complete this quest. If our framework for theology is to be a creative force without and within human life, we must confess some quality of humility concerning our grasp of this reality. If man's facility for comprehension is less than this creative force, then our understanding is never completed. This does not excuse us from the search. However, such a stance makes worship an exciting extension of this reach for God.

The focus of my quest for understanding and fleshing out the truth is the witness of Scripture. I know that many of my friends simply can't make this kind of leap of faith. They have been bitterly stung by the church's castration of Scripture in worship. It has been maimed by lame proclamation. Scripture has been gutted of power by misguided brothers and sisters who erroneously believe that freedom with the Bible displaces intellectual commitment. How do you celebrate theologically when you don't seek a fuller understanding of the source of your celebration?

Scripture as bench mark

The community of the people of God is still the cradle in which the Holy Spirit nurtures persons in understanding. This is not an escape into a "back to the Bible" simplicity. I make this kind of affirmation after having spent years channeling, chopping, and critically rearranging the biblical materials. Still this is the one source of tradition which can give us the freedom to experiment. The experimenter needs a bench mark. Scripture can be it. What does the term "celebration" really mean? It's used by everyone. The newspaper ad shouts, "sellebration." Americans have a terrible time finding a life-style of relaxation and celebration. A major magazine devoted a whole issue a couple years back to the problem of Americans in quest of leisure. They kill themselves in the process of speeding for rest. Our hobbies are strained. We usually justify them through the argument that they save us money. Why do we have to defend that which might turn us on?

The uptightness we celebrate during the week cannot easily be cast away to freely celebrate the love of God. Celebration is that leap of love which places us in a naked and bold confrontation with that which totally grasps us while renewing us. We can celebrate love's body. We can celebrate the pain and suffering of life. We can celebrate death. We can celebrate birth. However, we don't usually celebrate much from our life experience. Celebrating is dangerous. It exposes so much of our inner self. Celebrating also requires emotional energy. The electric man is tempted to turn from celebrating, in an interpersonal sense, because it demands so much surrender. We are delightfully spent after celebrating. Communion with God in the midst of brothers and sisters is a heady experience which overwhelms and changes.

Mountaintop or valley of action?

Where does one turn to gather the substance of the celebration of God? So much emotional energy is wasted by the saints who fight over the false dichotomy of church tradition versus the world. You know what I mean. It is the kind of thinking where a person wants to focus on the "pure Word of God." His antagonist wants to celebrate the pain and suffering of the world. They don't speak and can't authentically worship together. Authentic celebration of God always encompassed the God of life. Moses is not called into the pure truth of "mountaintop" theology. The incarnation of God's love can only be known as Moses celebrates his calling to deliver Israel from Egypt. This dual focus of worship undercuts some of the comfort factor which seems so important to modern worshipers. Indeed a close look at the witness of Scripture suggests that a lot of people were disturbed by the bite of God's confrontation with them. Where do the contemporary people of God find the confidence to be free in the biblical promise? The foundation of celebration frees man to bear the burden of human suffering and need in the context of worship.

Yet a person of faith cannot do authentic worship without a focus on God. If he can't focus on what the essence of the faith really is, he can't do what he is called to do in celebration. If Moses hadn't been able to hear the voice and see the bush, there would have been no focus for this act of celebration and worship.

What kind of God emerges from the mist? What kind of Jesus is real and meaningful to the worshiper? It seems that everybody will pick what he needs or wants when Jesus takes shape for him. A group of students interviewed people in the streets of a major city. They carried mounted pictures of a laughing Jesus. They asked people to comment on the picture. One lady said, "For a minute I thought that it was Jesus. This man, in the picture, however, has yellow teeth. Jesus didn't have yellow teeth!" Her Jesus would not have discolored teeth. He would have used the right toothpaste! Yet, we have to make our abstract concepts concrete. God has to take some shape for us. An old man with the beard serves as a useful way out. Can we really move beyond anthropomorphic imagery when attempting to deal personally with our conceptual basis for faith?

I must deal with these questions as I attempt to focus my direction of worship for August. These questions are inseparable from the givens of my people. How do we read the sensors of our people to know how they are seeking the shape and form of their God? If we see the people as vehicles of God's grace in human society, we must take them seriously. The writing on the wall may be written in characters—human characters. We have talked elsewhere about the importance of getting an early warning system to hear the nature of our people. What are some ways of accomplishing this?

Clergymen will always complain that there is not the kind of communication between themselves and the worshipers around the celebration experience that they would like. Cheap talk has been abundant concerning sermon "discussions." However, those preachers who really need such an input are afraid of it. At best these experiences tend to focus on the leader of worship. "How did you like the sermon?" is the wrong question. Worship is more than the sermon. Many clergymen will not accept this. Their whole reason for existence focuses on this preaching role. People want to hear a "good preacher." However, authentic celebration embraces the whole means of fleshing out the truth in community. The sermon may or may not play a significant part in this process. It should be possible in real celebration for the people not to notice who is the main enabler. Why can't a whole staff or a whole parish do liturgy together?

There should be a fuller process of intercommunication in the worship setting as it stands. It is so agonizing to see the eyes of people and to sense that things are happening within them. Yet, those reactions to the pursuit of the truth remain beyond the community that worships.

My decision for Christ and his church

It is hard to write about the process of doing and being theology. One can quite easily take provisional positions of faith. Our church or religious tradition gives us these premises without our real consent. It was different for me. I grew up without obvious theological structures. My mother and father brought to our family a mixed tradition (Protestant and Catholic). They gave me a basic ethical structure. However, the cracks in this system were not filled in by church school or continuous worship experience. My high school decision to join the church and become part of a theological community was important. However, there is so much I now reject of this early faith. The social stance of these important influences no longer seems to fit the theological structure built during the years that have passed. What happens when I lead worship with one stance and others worship with another outlook? Are there basic organizing factors that do bring us together as a people focused on the same God and same faith? Perhaps it doesn't make any difference. People will find what they want to find from a worship experience in spite of what the enablers think they are doing. When I am entrusted with convening the worship experience, do I impose my understanding of faith upon the people? How do I enable them to celebrate faith themselves?

Where are heads at?

There is something so subjective about worship. Good worship demands a lot from each person present. Being up front in the traditional setting is a big advantage. You can see eyes and note body language. There is so much going on even in the most placid setting. Why won't that lady look at me? Why is that man shaking his head in disagreement? I remember the former mental patient who told how her world of hope opened up during a communion service. It was the moment of preparation. Everyone had his head bowed in solemn confession. She was watching the clergyman. Their eyes met. He smiled slightly and winked! She said that suddenly a touch of humanity came flooding into her life. There was the flesh she needed for the words of hope and expectation, which until then had just been empty phrases.

I am always bothered when I can't perceive that something has happened in worship. Does the validity of celebration depend upon my acknowledgment of it? Are my expectations always so demanding that I am disappointed about reality? Must they meet the Christ I know or their own? Should he have yellow or sparkling white teeth?

It has bone in it— I just love it that way

Dr. William Herbert King was a gracious man. He not only released preaching potentiality from within the most timid student, but he was also a first-class cook. Marilyn and I were nervous to be entertaining in our student apartment a man we so respected. As we began dinner, the guest opened his baked potato to be met with the rock-like structure of uncooked potato. "That's the way I like it. It has bone in it. I just love it that way." He was helping us live with a bad situation. Many of us have been working too long in our attempt to live with bad situations of worship. We accept the rock-like structuring of celebration and say that this is the way we like it. Do worshipers always feel like opening with a joyous call to worship? Do we always feel like having confession at the same place in the service each week? Seminary classes in liturgy suggest flexibility in worship. Some professors use a shorthand to urge the students to be free. "Remember, you can celebrate by having ACTS, or CATS, or TACS." (A-Adoration; C-Confession; T-Thanksgiving; S-Sacraments). However, it is depressing to see what these students do with such a modest suggestion—nothing! The young worship leader is prone to play with the liturgy of his first charge upon his arrival. People are offended by change in this nostalgic dimension of their lives. He is quickly burned and learns better than to touch the worship area of his ministry.

"specials"

One of the most suggestive aspects of worship in the local setting is the special occasion. The church year is bursting with "specials." The seasons invite fresh forms of celebration. Most churches will give the restless a chance during Lent or Christmas. The Christmas pageants are really services for the fringe groups who have no representation within the church: the children and those who teach. Yet, even within this special context there is very little experimentation.

The occasion of worship is very important to the structure of what you are going to do. What happens Sunday morning must change the rhythm of what you do. When a service is really done by the worshiper, the form usually meets the resulting needs of the people quite naturally. If there has been a bad fight at the annual meeting, there should be some dealing with it at the time of celebration. What should confession mean when brothers and sisters have been at each other's throats? It is interesting that many of the practices of the small, rural churches of another age seem to build room for this kind of self-expression. The time when some would stand and bid the man in the congregation to direct prayers on behalf of his needs that week is now gone. However, that simple practice gets at what is being sought in some of the wildest liturgies.

People do liturgy

The inflexibility of the service structure usually reflects the rigidity of the worship leader. When you get right down to what happens in most Catholic, Protestant, and Jewish services, it is the clergyman who calls the shots. Because he is in this position alone he is very careful not to do something which will stir up the people who worship—unfortunately.

Structure then must follow the content of the word and the context of the worshiper. This content and context of salvation contains many aspects of faith and life. Some are meaningful and important at a given moment. These aspects must then be expressed. When there is a crying need for reconciliation, other facets of the history of salvation must take a back seat. They simply do.

You are a one-eyed Jack and I have seen your other eye

Dave and I saw *One Eyed Jacks* four times. It wasn't that we were Brando freaks. It was just the whole flick. I guess that we liked the overlay of character which seemed to represent all of us. We are good guys—good guys and bad guys—all at the same time. Just when we are trying to be one thing we deny our other self and turn out being inauthentic. However, we must know this overlay of becoming in order to communicate. Brando saw his former friend's "other eye." We knew what was going to happen concerning the situation. It would be a fight to the death.

When I go into Heinz Chapel, it will not be a shoot-out. However, it may be a life or death thing for all of us if we take our message and task at face value. Celebrating the actuality of claiming new life over the destructive old life is a key to how we are able to do the truth with our brothers and sisters.

How do I go to this celebration with any kind of reading as to where these folk will be? How do we really know where a person is? When I am caught in one of these situations I like to imagine who the worshipers might be. I fill up the place with cross sections of folk from my past. In this way I can probe for a form and message which will be true to the God who calls me to new life, and yet which will also be sensitive to his people. They are his flesh at this given moment.

Plugging John into all of this

Maybe John will be there. He is black and beautiful. He is a bundle of talent and feeling. Times have been hard for him. There are personal hassles of relationship which leave wounds still unhealed. Inside him there is a font of creative energy. He is musician, poet, philosopher, dancer, and man of faith. Each layer seems to strike out and hit people deeply. John is playing the last act of the academic game. He is teaching and finishing up that degree which will give him a rainbow future. At least, that is what the educational tracking system has told him during these years of slavery.

John is the kind of guy who often leads celebrations himself. I have seen him turn all of us on to life and the Good News. He believes in the communion of touch. The body is to be celebrated. If I choose to use the idiom of touch and body language will this be most meaningful to him?

My mind is flashing with input from other celebrations where the beautiful surrender of the body to God played an important role. The Song of Solomon celebrates the joy of the body. In fact, this book is not often mentioned in our religious education. We simply don't know what to do with it. Even the elaborate allegorical interpretations of the book don't seem to work. Who feels very satisfied with the explanation that the praise of the beauty of the beloved's breast really refers to Moses and Aaron? This kind of handling of Scripture does not even make those who are uptight about the body very comfortable.

There is recurring criticism about the sensual age in which we live. The electric environment itself makes us more sensually aware than ever before. There are more opportunities to have the senses continually massaged. Yet, again it is clear that people are denying what is being urged upon them religiously and culturally—to become the embodiment of truth. The incarnation is an aspect of the faith which should be celebrated. It is more than a Christmas idea. Whatever finally emerges from the composition as a valid understanding of the church in our day will have to be overlayed with a realization of what the body of Christ really means for us.

"Pass the peace"

Passing the peace is a common expression of body language which harks back to the early church practice of the kiss of peace. This is still celebrated as part of the tradition by several communions. It is amazing to see the kind of response John has had when he attempts to free his brothers and sisters to enjoy their bodies. Hands will be withdrawn quickly or not extended at all. Creative Christian educators Jan and Ed Jepson have incorporated several body features into what they call the "sacrament of penance." Just the process of exploring each other's hands can be a means of understanding forgiveness and acceptance. Al Johnson developed an extensive church union service which focused on the body language of washing feet. This biblical practice enabled a diverse group of people to find communion and the love of each other.

Jerry Kerns

My mind jumps back to last summer. I remember the worship experience we had with eighty young people and adults in Kentucky. Jerry Kerns and the other brothers and sisters explored ways by which we could use body language to worship and celebrate. Our experience included a midnight walk barefoot through the wet grass. We had spent some time doing a sense awareness exercise with hands. We then held hands and with eyes closed snaked our way around the seminary, down the back stairs of the chapel, and into the basement. We had to depend on the language of our neighbor's body to overcome these obstacles. We were communing with each other in our quest to worship God. A communion service with the body and blood of Christ interfaced the experience of our corporate body language. What trust and interdependence these couple of hours created!

Dancing?

John has done a lot of dancing. He has used the movement of the body to create an experiential web of celebration and worship. I have been part of a group of worshipers slowly moving as a Psalm is being read. What a fantastic way to let the Scripture really get into you. For just a few minutes the joyous worship at the ancient temple of the Hebrews could be felt. We have also done less dramatic bodily things. As the worshipers experienced the multimedia prayer of intercession, they were asked to join hands. After the shocking three minutes of visual and audio suffering, they were asked to respond by sharing what feelings their neighbors had experienced through the hand of their neighbor concerning our role in the prayer of intercession.

In one worship experience that comes back to mind, the worshipers were given a rope. They each held onto a part of it. In the course of the experience they were made aware again and again that it was a corporate experience. The sway and rhythm of the group became part of everyone's experience. Sometimes we have asked people to feel the pulse beat of their

Body as a medium of worship

George V. McCausland

neighbor's wrist while the prayer of intercession and petition is made. This is to remind them that it is on behalf of the need of every person that these prayers are directed. As they experience the heartbeat of another body, they participate intimately with another's concern.

I remember an occasion where we were struggling to design a small group worship where we could utilize the body as a medium of worship to God. We designed a benediction where one person went around to each person from the back and placed his hands on the shoulders of the worshiper. He slowly pronounced a personal benediction with the laying on of his hands. Of course, the practice of laying on of hands is not new. It is a biblical means of commissioning healing, forgiving, and loving. George V. McCausland tells many stories of healing services where people lay hands of love upon each other.

As I ramble through my thoughts concerning the celebration I am planning for John, a sudden memory of last winter comes to mind. I was coming home late at night. I had ridden the iron horse (one of the last trolleys in the country) home. A neighbor lady was getting off the trolley at the same time. A fresh snow covered the ground. It was cold and slippery. As we started walking toward our homes, she gently slipped her hand around my arm. A very small gesture. It would have been quite natural during the early years of the American society. However, it suggests a fresh relationship of mutual support. How do we get this kind of basic human warmth into the climax of celebration in worship? It is so tragic to think how little we use our bodies for mutual celebration at the very time that God calls for full communal commitment to him.

The given that hits me about the Heinz Chapel event is that the seats are nailed to the floor. The seating there and elsewhere is really designed to suppress intimacy. We can't move and pick up the vibrations from each other. It seems that church seating design even makes the participation in the sacraments difficult unless everyone remains seated. The body is put on ice until you leave most worship settings.

Rob McClure

On one occasion Rob McClure and I tied people together for a celebration event. We wanted to give them the experience of communion between people as they underwent communion with God. Their bodies became joined at the wrists. The ribbon bond gave them new awareness of how we are truly one body. There was also that summer event where we tied people together and then cut them apart in the course of the service. The piece of rope that held them now became a single bracelet. Later this body ornament was exchanged as an offering of love to one another.

Community dancing is being done by a lot of folk in this kind of celebration which incorporates the body. The music or reason for dancing is most important. Rock music formats particularly suggest that such participation be undertaken. Again all these ideas must be based on the life-style and needs of our people. It would not be fitting to ask a group of aged people to dance. Even though many would love to do it, it may be physically too difficult for them.

Movement within a worship setting is a kind of body language which contributes a lot to an authentic worship celebration. However, in many Protestant churches there is very little movement by the people. At one time there used to be the closing altar call which gave some of the brothers and sisters a chance to move. People even stood up and added to the common prayers. However, mainline churches do not have such movement anymore.

Balloons, etc.

Let's assume in my speculation that John may particularly want to celebrate joy. How can movement flesh out the joy of the religious tradition? Perhaps the dimension of thanksgiving could be utilized as the expression of joy. We might explore the participatory probes of Corita Kent and others. They have helped "happenings" to unfold. This approach to worship releases the possibilities for each participant to celebrate freely the joy within him in response to the promise of faith. They may give the people a bag of things which they can freely use as they move around and celebrate. Perhaps you drape crepe paper on your neighbor to express joy. Balloons are blown up and bounced about. Kent Schneider has even used the movement of the mouth to help people celebrate! For a youth conference he passed out bubble gum. As they chewed and blew bubbles, he explored the shape and change of human life.

If we are going to have joy in this service, we will need to explore the pain and suffering we know in our lives. The Christian faith doesn't permit a glossing over of our wounded. The suffering must be recognized so that the healing can take place. How do you openly explore such suffering with a large group of people from different backgrounds? Perhaps there can be some way of sharing these needs through a projection technique. In one retreat setting we passed a newspaper around and asked each person to rip out a section of the page. We then asked the people to study the piece of paper carefully in order to find something which reflects the suffering and pain of our world. We then shared what they had found; this was done again in terms of joy. There might be a sharing which can be done in a personal way to the person next to you. Each person whispers some of the pain and suffering which keeps joy from being fully known. Each person then gives his neighbor words of assurance concerning the real source of joy.

Another way of getting into this aspect of the faith for John would be to use some of the work of Jack Ridl. Jack has asked people for random words which express sorrow for them. He then fashions these words into a poetic form before their eyes. They then break this new art form into a responsive reading. This is done several times and in several ways. This technique is analogous to the old idea of having a congregation sing ''rounds.''

We could also build upon a dramatic foundation and evolve a dialogue between someone in the congregation and one or more of the leaders. The dialogue could be a debate. Maybe the person in the congregation could suddenly jump up and complain about this talk about suffering when people really want hope and joy. This would release the energies and questions within many others.

As I think back over these probes, I realize how hard it is to know those worshipers. Have I really pegged some of the worship dimensions important to my friend John? What about the other people who are not concerned with movement? Maybe they are uptight about their bodies. Maybe they don't want to touch or be touched by anybody or anything. What other obstacles to joy are blocking other people's minds and spirits? How will any of these ideas unlock the access to endless action and rest? How do we get to see that ''other eye'' in order to move to the celebration of worship?

And then you use a yellow bowl

Margaret

I will never forget Margaret. She represents so much that is important about faith and worship. When I must speculate about a worship experience for an unknown group of people, I always know that there will have to be some there like her. I pray that there will!

She is a remarkable person. She is a lot of different things wrapped up in one huge, warm bundle. Her life is structured to care for people. She does this quite literally as a practical nurse. No, she is more than this. Margaret actually does much of the management in a home for aged people. Yet, she is paid very little. You know, there are always people like this around. They are not appreciated the way they should be. Her love and care is fantastic. She just seems to have that special quality that knows how to reach inside another person's heart and stroke gently that place where the rub of life is hurting.

She is the staying power of her family. For a number of complex reasons she carries the load. Her faith is very basic. Jesus Christ is the Lord of her life. It was embarrassing to be her pastor and see how she would give and give of her meager income for the work of the local church. She would give more than the hotshot family which massaged the humble institution for political benefit and took the credit for everything. At times of special need, she would always slip in extra funds to see that the poor, hungry, or dehumanized got help. She served on the ruling board of our church. She was there when the pastor felt called to go to Selma. The people were uptight by this participation in this nonviolent (Seems ironic now, doesn't it?) witness. I suspect that this kind of social involvement was not her personal style of taking the gospel into life. However, the board supported the pastor's proposal to take the trip. Margaret stood firmly behind him.

She liked to eat. Her bulk showed the results of this indulgence. She cooked all kinds of things. There was one recipe which has been handed down through generations. It was for a special kind of bread. Only Margaret and a few other souls seemed to be able to bake it properly. She would dutifully explain all the ingredients of this special delight. She would conclude the outline of the process with the last factor: ". . . and then you use a yellow bowl." Most people would dismiss the last comment or just laugh. However, in secret, she would say that it was the use of her mother's yellow mixing bowl that made the recipe work. How do you enable a celebration to happen for a person like this? How do you include a "yellow bowl" or the tradition in such a way that the service is faithful to the past and the present?

Communion of saints

Yes, there will be Margarets there. They represent, in the best sense, what the church has called the communion of saints. They are the embodiment of the history of salvation for which we have gathered for celebration. Worship cannot be celebration without a sense of what has happened in the past. The historical dimension to the faith enactment plays a key role in making worship happen. One cannot understand the working of the Holy Spirit unless a sense of what he has done in the past is present. When we grapple for real, immediate, experiential worship experience we can easily confuse the novel with the authentic. The power of the Holy Spirit is not the buzz or zing of getting high for the moment. The deep reality of the Holy Spirit working among his gathered folk is that the now is an extension of what has happened from the beginning to the end.

As we have probed earlier in our quest for worship, history and nostalgia are not to be confused. Margaret liked old hymns and familiar language. However, she was more together than to be satisfied with the trappings of old. She could weave the promise and call of the past into the fabric of the now. The escape from Egypt and the deliverance from Selma had to be eternally related in her mind. She could not give her body to Selma, but her spirit was responsive to both. It is unfortunate that so many brothers and sisters who work among folk like Margaret don't realize the gifts to be shared by such folk for now needs.

Gospel Hymns

It was always hard to bring the gifts and needs of my Margarets to fruition through worship. Do I use older forms in a new way? Perhaps I could use the Gospel hymns with new words? Or do I project the words of the hymns she sings by heart on the wall next to slides of contemporary parallels? This would give her the experiences of saying the familiar, but having the new demands visually reinforced. Perhaps Margaret's character suggests to me that I use a very standard order of worship and within it use fresh ways of coming at the basic elements. For instance, this might mean that I could have the Call to Worship changed from the worship enabler saying opening sentences. A biblical injunction to worship could be passed by whisper from one person to the next. Each person in this way summons his neighbor to worship.

Prayer of Confession

The prayer of confession could move from the typical written word to some means of personal involvement. We have too often assumed that by having a group of people read somebody's words together we are having community response. Nowhere in our society do we currently use this kind of unison response as a meaningful experience. The few other places where we do say a pledge or recite with others are old traditions which mean very little to most participants. The church has persisted in this practice without acknowledging the electric age's influence. Some liturgical reformists have changed words. Hip liturgies may use street language. Others have created clever restatements of the older prayers. However, I suspect that this is nonproductive. The Margarets may feel uncomfortable confessing in a language not familiar and not their own. The restless church member may appreciate the meaningful language, but he is still being asked to undertake an exercise unnatural to his life-style.

Are there some liturgical postures which reach back and reach ahead? Can Margaret's given frame of faith be tapped while carrying her into the present context where truth must be done? Perhaps people could write out sins for which forgiveness must be asked. These could be gathered and used as the basis of bidding prayers. A few churches are establishing prayer boards upon which matters of prayer can be posted and then integrated into the service. The forms of the prayers are somewhat familiar and yet the content is contemporary from the worshiper's perspective.

The whole realm of confession must be examined carefully by those struggling with contemporary worship. The matter of individual confession of sin to brothers and sisters must find a new medium. The world is filled with people moving through life without any sense of forgiveness. People are more sensitive about their sins against God and neighbor than most religious leaders imagine. How do we tap into this area of celebration and lance the infected area with the message of forgiveness through Christ? Each person in a secure community of brothers and sisters could even confess individually in a whisper to the person next to him. The person could then utter words of assurance of pardon which the faith gives. For small groups we have dug into the tradition of confession as an inseparable part of worship by passing a mirror before each worshiper. Each person is asked to confess something about which he or she is ashamed as reflected in the mirror. Pardon is assured through touching the head and uttering a biblical statement about such grace.

Petition and intercession

How do we enter into the realm of the prayers of petition and intercession? A list of unfamiliar people often used by clergymen is not enough. Some communions use portions of Scripture read responsively as a means to cover these and other prayer areas. I know that Margaret would be most concerned about the areas of worship concerning the needs of her family and others in the world. Her giving and personal service indicate this high priority. However, I suspect that most Sundays she knew about more suffering and human need from her work than I did. How can I suggest to her the areas of real concern? Somehow I have to let her fill in the needs. If people could be enabled just to stand and share, this would be great. However, we have left that era of worship experience in most of our large services. Some churches have regular pulpit assistants or liturgists who do the prayers. However, the layman called to do what the minister or clergyman has always done doesn't make it any better. The whole caring energy of the group must be tapped. How can Margaret share with us her lonely and bleeding patients? How can we know her inward worries about her family?

Perhaps we can meet her needs by carefully using certain seasons of the year or rhythms of life. Most churches have special music or a special sermon on the holiday Sundays. However, maybe we should reshape the traditional elements of the service for Margaret into a vessel capable of carrying the load that needs to be celebrated. What happens in the service nearest Memorial Day? Death and dying have special meanings for Margaret. She helps people face pain and suffering. What does Easter mean theologically for her? How do the old and familiar take on new meaning for her in terms of her work? How do we provide strength for her when she must assist in keeping someone alive by means which totally dehumanize the patient?

Offering

The offering is important to her also. This is a significant way by which she can express herself as a woman of faith. Maybe the gifts of offering should be presented in a different way by those who give. Some traditions have the gifts of money given as the people walk out and make this the first act as they reenter the world. One friend of mine develops special rituals by which people make special gifts of silver by coming down front and placing the coins on the table. There is a very fuzzy picture in the minds of most worshipers concerning what really happens to the money given each week. Most churches simply do not communicate in human terms the kind of work done on behalf of their people. I believe that a faithful people of God will support any authentic work that they understand. The moment of giving should be celebrated fittingly. How can the source (faith in God) and object (work of ministry) of such an act be highlighted in such a way that the participant really participates?

Margaret will also be looking in worship for the bench mark of her faith: the Bible. It is amazing how few services really provide such a base. Some people may assume that the Bible's use leads only to dry and bloodless faith. However, the role of the Bible is important to those who want to flesh out the faith in social action. The Bible's poor reputation is based on its widespread misuse in the worship experience. Even in the traditions which claim a central role for Scripture there have been some sad applications. There may be the preacher who takes six months to preach his way through one book of the Bible. He takes three or four words at a time and builds his message from this limited context. Such an approach also places the Scripture only in the narrow confines of the sermon. In other settings the Bible is just tacked on some place in a topical sermon. Maybe the whole thrust of a service could be biblical. In one retreat setting 250 young people prepared for worship by acting out Genesis 1 in small tribal groups. They were back in Eden and had to build a new world—without using the English language! They were to bring messages back to the community celebration to communicate to the other tribes.

The Scripture is basic to Margaret's faith. She must be challenged to "put the Scripture on." We should approach Scripture together. Somehow in this chapel service I must draw upon the Scriptural orientation of the Margarets who will be there.

Dealing with someone like this woman means that even the final encounter with her has to be meaningful. Instead of just saying good morning while the worshiper mumbles something about "good sermon," we might do something to strengthen what has been proclaimed. I usually "press the flesh" (sorry about that, former President Johnson). I take the worshiper's hand in both of mine and say "the peace of God be with you." I try to give out as much as possible so the person at the door feels the encounter between two people.

Embracing

A number of creative worship leaders like to use an even more intimate parting gesture. They like to embrace after each worship event. This is an extension of the kiss of peace which apparently was practiced in sections of the church during the early years. I know that this might appeal to Margaret. It would have to be real. In fact, she warmly embraced me the last time we said good-bye in the church narthex several years ago. It was a beautiful moment. It told me so much about what we had been celebrating together those three years.

One intimidating aspect of creative liturgy for those who have traditional people is the leader's limited view of history. He will mistake custom for history. A hard look at the history of liturgy will stagger the investigator. Almost everything has been tried somewhere by worshiping men. You will find your latest idea if you keep looking. The offering, for instance, has been received in a variety of approaches. Brothers and sisters, well and sleeping, have sacrificed anything from beautiful maidens to credit cards. Second-century Gnostic Christians talked about a sacrament of the bridal chamber. Some local communities have added football games to their "sacramental" concern. You are only limited and misled by your mind. This kind of perspective should also encourage the worshiping animal to realize that innovation is traditional. It is just that we get caught in one frozen frame of history's moment and can't compute the flow and rhythm which links us with the past.

I must admit that I do have moments of concern about Margaret and her folk. Will they fully understand what I am trying to do with her in mind? There is always the chance that she will not be able to translate the fresh forms as extensions of her faith. Perhaps I should build in some alternatives for her within the service. The service will have to be participatory in such a way that I can get a reading of what is happening while it happens. She should be respected enough to have ways by which she can hold back if the situation becomes too threatening. My main mind-set is one of love and concern for her. It is not my task to "blow her mind" for the sake of being "far out." I do feel that the incarnate Word of God does this to us in itself. There is a fine balance between being faithful to this explosive content and to the worshiper who desires to be plugged into this kind of celebration. How do they meet? How do we play our role of mediator in the situation? When do we let the content do its work and when do we bear the responsibility to the worshiper and to the Word?

Margaret deserves so much. She demands so much by the nature of the faith she bears. I remember one Sunday when I was uncomfortable about the message I was to preach shortly. It was one of those Amos Sundays; you know, the kind of message that cuts deep into the indifference we allow to build up in our lives. I saw her coming in the door. She noted that I seemed a bit uncomfortable. I told her that the message which possessed me this week was a hard one to bear. She asked me if I felt that it had to be celebrated. I said that I thought it must be faced. She told me to have confidence in what I was called to speak. I knew that the message would be hard on all of us. It would rip into parts of her life and call her to be more and do more. Yet, she had given me encouragement to do the truth as it struck my role of responsibility.

God bless you, Margaret

The kind of support that the Margarets of your life can give is fantastic! They can give the person of another mind-set the kind of authenticity to himself that he may not have. Maybe this kind of interpersonal validation between brothers and sisters is one of the most important factors of worship. It is such a tragedy that most contemporary worship does not bring about this kind of recognition. Very little communion between the persons of

God can be experienced in most corporate worship events. The actualization that the traditionalist, the reformist, the uptight, the strung out, the tranquilized, and the turned on are together in one place is the gospel taking flesh! Yet, Margaret and hippies are usually not brought into this kind of relationship through the worship event. They are usually left to get what they want from the service and go their separate ways, each person disliking what may have turned on the neighbor. If you are my brother or sister, it is essential that I know and love what turns you on! The ultimate concern of your life has importance for me because it is your essence. It is that part of God which has been received and made flesh by you. This sometimes becomes a hard quest. Each of us comes to the worship experience with certain boundaries. In some way our life experience leaves us with the conviction that for us there must be a "yellow bowl" to properly fulfill our recipe for faith and life.

I am a Zen-Presbyterian

Jacinta

The needs and gifts of Jacinta are different. She comes from a broader world than most of my friends. Her faith realm embraces many rich traditions. She has fleshed out the faith in many different contexts. She has spent many hours in the coffee houses of working-class German youth. Jacinta has brought warmth and love into the heart of American slums. This woman of faith and of the world has also helped suburban nomads find routes to faith options. Her whole thrust of existence involves the quest to have men of faith live and love together. "Ecumenical" is really too limited a term to describe her perspective.

If she were going to be present at the service I am planning, I would have to consider a number of things about her as a person. She is bright. She reads a lot. Jacinta tries to understand and do theology. It will be important for me to realize that she is a European. She speaks several languages. This woman has experienced worship in just about every possible setting. How do these factors influence the structuring and emphasis of this service? How can I meet her needs and strengths in such a way that the content of our worship will meet her and she will meet it?

She knows many liturgical traditions. She should be able to interweave different forms to plug into her faith system. It won't be hard for her to understand the reasoning or source of our liturgical probes. Yet, I think that she is a woman of simplicity. I know that she is easily moved to feel the pain of others. I remember one afternoon when we were eating in a restaurant and sharing ourselves in conversation. I told the story of suffering experienced when I was a hospital chaplain. A small child had died after heart surgery. The father of the child pulled all of us out of tears and despair by assuring us that their dead child had taught us how to love. "Many parents never learn this." Jacinta shed tears over this real story of human pain and strength. This is the kind of immediate and sensitive person she is.

Catholic and Protestant

With her present we must dip into a kind of structure which will permit a sharing of individual gifts and needs. Al Johnson was involved in an ecumenical venture which effectively drew people together from different backgrounds. He used music and dancing as a means of having people participate in the celebration of community. Jacinta's being Roman Catholic makes me remember the breadth of faith when I utter the name of Jesus Christ. If I am in him and he is in me, then I am in every brother and sister who has the same kind of relationship. Jacinta is my sister and we must enact that in our celebration at the end of summer. Some of my neo-Pentecostal friends end their spirit-filled evening of celebration by having people identify what tradition they represent. It is amazing to see the broad face of God working in human life as he touches people everywhere. The book of Acts reminds us that this is how it all began.

Acts 2:1-4 might be a good way to think through the aspect of worship forced upon us by the possible participation of this friend of mine. The passage is so basic to worship in any setting. The fact that the apostles were together in one place suggests that it was this kind of transpersonal power which was the occasion for which the Spirit came. To me this does not demand emotionalism. It does compel us to have experiential worship. We must do and experience that which we often resolve into mere words. We must dip into the realm of the senses. What does the essence of our religious history as persons have to say about how we feel and think?

In our geographical area this means that we cannot have the sacrament of the Lord's Supper together as Protestants and Catholics. As Jacinta has

It hurts to be at separate tables!

said, "Perhaps it is necessary to experience a time of aching for this kind of sharing before we know the reality of it." What would happen if we built in some of the aching? Perhaps we could reach a point where we could go no further and somehow know what is before us and yet not complete it. We do not celebrate the whole spectrum of Christian theology in much of our liturgy. Good Friday may enable us to peek into the role of suffering and the cost of discipleship. However, much of our message is pitched toward comfort and immediate solutions to the problems we pose. The history of salvation isn't this way. Moses is faithful to his calling even when he knows that he must pine for a land of milk and honey without getting there. There is such longing for the reality to come. Yet, in this celebration of reaching there is also acknowledgment that the future is now. What we do—what we celebrate—is undertaken for its own worth. We cannot judge the quality of our life together as a worshiping people according to the standards of the world. As Dietrich Bonhoeffer has reminded us, "It is not the purpose and the commission of the church to preach the Gospel on its fingers." (*The Way to Freedom*, Vol. II, Harper and Row, 1966, p. 78). This is not a justification for boring worship which is endured for the sake of faithfulness. However, people's reaction to Christ should remind us that theological celebration is not a trumpet blast which calls everyone. In fact, there are those who will be summoned, but who will not respond. They may walk out or just sleep through it all. We may love each other in worship, but still feel the pain of not being able to consummate it.

What Jacinta keeps reminding me by her love and broad outreach when I place her in this worship communion is that there has never been a time so ripe for our kind of community with God and our neighbor. This is a bit ironic. We are in a time of drastic decline in the institutional church's power to reach out. The gum and bailing wire will not save us from ourselves. Those who come are there to rest. Those who don't come are restless for what celebration of faith gives.

Time is near!

This kind of hopeful hopelessness keeps emerging among the folk who are doing celebration with people. They rest in the bosom of faith and face the judgment which is coming. This duality permits honesty concerning what the Beatles used to call "the great fall." They knew that the success game would finally get them and it would be different after that from what it had been before. The church is just entering its period of the "great fall." However, this is not necessarily bad. Jacinta bears the witness of a great new birth of faith-people everywhere. The ability to be hopeless and hopeful has allowed a lot of us to pool the reality of our situations and then go on from there. Together we now discover new meanings of faith and new forms through which to celebrate the moment. Our celebration and worship are inseparable from our work and life together. Perhaps this is why events such as the once-only chapel service which is the occasion of my meandering about worship tend to be so hollow. What Jacinta typifies in my mind is not a shallow "take a Christian to worship" kind of ecumenical effort. Celebration with Jacinta and my other brothers and sisters is a manifestation of the reality acknowledged concerning Jesus Christ. Celebration is the outgrowth of present and past reality in the lives of the worshipers.

The occasion of ecumenically sensitive worship is usually the unusual. At this shaky point in mutual trust and understanding, the local people of faith will venture out on the occasion of Lent, Christmas, Thanksgiving, Youth Week, or something of the sort. Unfortunately a number of these token bids toward celebrating the reality of oneness in Christ have been going on at this level for years. The timidity and ineffectiveness of these events are usually compounded by dragging in the mass media as a last thought. Radio is the medium usually saddled with three hours on Good Friday. A series of speakers give forth on their thoughts about a general theme (the last words of Christ is the all-time favorite). The shortcomings of these kinds of worship expressions for mass media man are numerous. Besides being bad radio and bad worship for the two conflicting communities (inside and outside the actual worship setting) it is also a fragmented means of celebration.

Tom McLaren has experimented with numerous means of using radio for this kind of ecumenical worship experience. One Good Friday he used the playlist of WJET (Erie) and tailored a three-hour format. The pop songs were familiar ones which in some way reflected upon suffering and pain. In between the records he used materials that he had gathered and recorded especially for the show. At the station he produced four one-minute spots. He simply collected bits and pieces (a top-forty song, documentary voice tracks, sounds, and his voice). He used the Dion song which was riding high on the charts ("Abraham, Martin, and John"). Tom dissected it into four sections (Lincoln, Martin Luther King, John and Robert Kennedy). He combined their actual voices (except Lincoln), a sound of a shot, music, and the concluding remark "Good Friday keeps happening all the time." This Good Friday special really hit the area hard. The comments were very favorable. People from many different backgrounds read the basic sound of the station with the theological meaning added. The "glue" between the records changed the meaning and thrust of the material heard by the listeners.

The kind of ecumenical reality to which Jacinta has committed her life is more than bits and pieces from different places which remain scrambled. Those leading worship must be able to draw upon a togetherness as folk so that the end results reflect this. I know reservations about such generalizations must pop into your mind. Men and women of the same tradition can't even sit down as brothers and sisters around the Word of God. However, such pettiness is just another sign of the end. The kind of probing we are doing is based on the hopeful hopelessness that must undergird us in the race to the end.

Jacinta is gentle. She is loving. Our worship experience designed with her faith in mind must slip into the character of this person. She can ride on the wings of enthusiasm and vigor when she sees that it wells up from a genuine source. Why are you doing this? Why are you doing it in this way?

My mind flashes back to another ecumenical service. Four hundred teen-agers gathered in the ballroom of a downtown hotel. After weeks of planning, a group of young people from a mixed bag of backgrounds came up with this design. The theme was: "Will the real Jesus please stand up?" A circular setting was chosen. A plaster statue of the head of Jesus had been made by one of the young people. The service began with a man wheeling the covered form onto the platform. He then walked off. During the course of the next ninety minutes clusters of people entered the central worship center and raised questions and suggested answers concerning what manner of person this man was. Each group did something to the statue to leave its understanding of it behind. One of the black groups came on the stage with chains and toy guns. They gave a powerful fifteen-minute recital of the history of slavery in the United States. They painted half of Jesus'

Plaster Jesus

52

face black, and he bore chains and the Black Panther symbol when they left. Music from the religious and pop culture provided transitions. The experience was concluded by the acknowledgment that all these points of view were really part of the Christ we follow. He had come to be with all of man. A love feast of cookies and punch took place as baskets and trays were passed around from person to person. Catholic and Protestant, conservative and liberal had a few minutes of celebration together. They had each contributed their faith to the faith feast.

Jacinta's presence at the celebration adds new dimensions to the demands upon me as the enabler. One evening at a speaking engagement one of the unhappy participants in the media presentation on change and theology asked, "What kind of a minister are you?" The question was loaded with all kinds of implications. I took it humorously. "I am a Zen-Presbyterian." There was a long moment of silence. He had taken it at face value. "What kind of a Presbyterian is that?" I had to spend fifteen minutes getting out of that smart remark. Jacinta has reinforced me. She has helped me to realize once again that there is a blur of distinction between those of us from different backgrounds who are brothers and sisters. Perhaps we should be hyphenating our labels a lot more. I suspect that we will be in the near future.

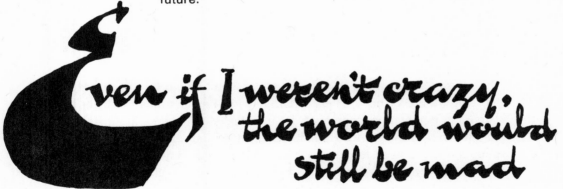

Even if I weren't crazy, the world would still be mad

Tom

Tom is my friend. We have known each other for several years. He was a high school student when we first met. I can't remember where. He did radio shows with me. Mostly we have talked in my living room or office. We were drawn together by a number of strange factors. Tom proudly claimed to be one of the three socialists in the area. He reads everything about political systems. Socialism is his area of expertise. He knew that he could come and we could talk about political and social options. It didn't make any difference that we agreed sometimes and disagreed other times. We could relax and just be ourselves.

"I have gone crazy." I could tell that the voice at the other end of the phone was shaky. Tom had been at the "college of his choice" for one day. Then the world came apart. He was returned to Pittsburgh and placed in a mental institution. It took six months in the hospital, twice a week sessions with his "shrink," and four pills a day to get him back on the street. We rap a lot about the process of getting yourself back together.

In the bottom of his despair he once told me that he knew that he was crazy. However, what bothered him so much was that even if he were sane the world would still be mad. That really hit me. Yes, he was right. Uptight power people will continue to get us into wars, depressions, and police states. This is only madness. How do you rebuild your broken life when you have seen the nature of life and you know it won't change? What kind of theology speaks to you from such a perspective?

Tom won't go for the "pie-in-the-sky" bit. He has tried the extra-church youth enthusiast groups. "They are so anti-intellectual. They won't let you use your mind." He knows that those political utopias are fantasy. He can't swallow religious dream pictures.

If Tom were to come to this chapel event, what would be the context of worship fitting for him? There would have to be some head in it for him. His mind demands engagement. He also lacks confidence in himself and his relationship to the world. He is caught in the pinch between caring about people and the need to care for himself. Tom would need a celebration which could recognize the evils of racism, war, male chauvinism, and the police state. He is also wired into the giant electric nerve ending environment. What aspects of celebration touch him?

This might be an ideal place for the use of electric media to flesh out suffering and the needs of God's creation. The use of visual materials is particularly helpful in this area. Many people are doing "multimedia liturgies.'' Literally hundreds of these celebrations have been built around Simon and Garfunkel material or *Jesus Christ Superstar.* I must keep Tom in mind and pick up a clue that his needs give us. He is sick. He is struggling to establish his identity apart from the electric world. These two realms tend to merge for him. He can't find himself in the intermix.

Overkill by media overload

Those who are experimenting with electric media tend to go for the kill. They overload their people with too much. They may use six slide projectors for forty minutes. The sound track is usually music—song after song with the pictures coming at every angle and speed. David Leachman tells about this danger. He reports that overload struck a number of people at a celebration the Power and Light Company put together. It contained two parts. Part one was a mind-blowing presentation of suffering. In part two they let the Beatles' song ''Here Comes the Sun'' carry the worshipers into hope and love. Although the two sections were of equal length, most people claimed that they couldn't feel hope after the biting power of the first half. More often people are knocked out of their seats by the awesome power of these productions. They then don't know what to do with the raw feelings inside them. We must pull hope and pain together in order to help Tom deal with his needs and the hope of the gospel.

Another temptation with the media experience is that it is placed before the group as if it is a show. Even the screen doesn't usually fit into the setting. Equipment often tends to get in the way of the audience.

Kent Schneider

However, Kent Schneider and his friends are a good example of what might be done with media in such a context. During one of their Lenten celebrations they used film, light, organ, slides, and artifacts to enable the people to participate in the suffering of Christ's people everywhere all the time. Kent and troupe used the basic structure of the usual worship service to open up the people to making their contributions to this corporate event.

Another group of creative worship enablers created an event in which the electric media became a key factor in their participation. They divided the group into three different viewing groups. The same sound track was used, but each group saw a single screen with different visual stimuli. One area viewed a series of traditional Sunday school pictures moving very slowly. (Actually it was a filmstrip cut into sections and mounted as slides.)

Another screen bore projections of pictures taken in their community. All the restaurants, homes, and points of beauty were shown. The third screen poured out quickly paced slides of pictures taken from magazines: war pictures, ads, and civil strife. After the input of this seeing and hearing extension of the electric sermon, the people were immediately asked to respond. What did you see about suffering of the world? People groped to express what their individual experiences were. Slowly the differences began to develop from their descriptions. Totally different orientations to the pain of the world emerged. The three screens were quickly replaced and the whole group heard the same sound track and saw all three screens at once. Again they were asked to respond to the Word of God. This time they were asked to share the hope of the situations. Where is the gospel in these contexts?

Nonverbal expression

Another way to interface worship and electric media is to expose the worshipers to a short input (ten to twelve minutes), then get a nonverbal response to what they felt. Perhaps they draw with crayons about their feelings. They are then asked to make their offering to God in the presence of their neighbors by holding up their drawings. The other people are asked to comment on them. This way the participant can project his feelings and not be threatened by having to verbalize his feelings. After the discussion, which is conducted as an offering, it is suggested that the experience be undertaken once again. Several people are picked at random from the worshipers. Each person is given one of the controls to the slide projector. The sound track is played and the people move the pictures along as they wish. They are told to do it in such a way that hope is found in what will be seen on the screen. It is amazing how new meanings can be found. Of course, the meanings are really in the minds and hearts of those who respond to what they want to see. Such an approach is very participatory and people-centered.

I start with sound

Sound tracks for such shows are easy to create. I usually begin with the sound. I try to put music, voice tracks, various sounds, and humor into my mixes. One easy way of creating such audio dimensions for worship is to take one song and expand it. There are a number of songs which are very vague and theologically suggestive. One has only to tape the song and with a razor blade cut it into sections. Using splicing tape (very inexpensive from audio centers), one need only add new sections of sound previously recorded. By using this piecemeal approach, you make a nice tight sound track for the media show. Most media freaks know all the tricks of creating slides. I describe many of these probes in *Let It Run* (John Knox Press, 1971, Side Two, p. 40), among them, the technique of making transparencies (slide film) from magazines (on clay-based paper—shiny) by using clear contact shelving material. You can also cut up filmstrips and make them into slides without damaging the usefulness of the original material. Even the cheapest cameras now have attachments for copping photos from magazines.

It is imperative that you move away from the slide shows of last summer's vacation, but not too close to a light show. People like Tom and Margaret simply couldn't assimilate the latter and would be bored by the former. In multimedia presentations for worship you are limited only by your imagination. You should be limited, however, by the needs of your people and the thrust of your content. The media have a way of carrying the creator away. I have been into such trips. It is still hard to bring it all down to a manageable level. Be aware, but don't be afraid. It is easier and harder than you can imagine.

One possibility for the use of multimedia in worship suggested by the techniques described above is that each person could make his own slide. If we had a bit of freedom in the worship setting, we could read the Scripture passage a number of times while each person, in silence, finds a magazine picture and makes a slide with the shelving paper process. The slides could then be placed in slide mounts and put into the projectors. The whole collection of slides would be shown while the passage is read again. For the sermon we could show each slide one at a time and have the person who made it raise his hand. Then the other people would comment on why they think he chose to make that particular slide to express his reaction to the passage.

TV spots

Multimedia also suggest mixture. You might mix into the slides a piece of film. TV commercials are fantastic (Check out your local station.). Also old news footage can make strong points for the worshiper. I have found that one must be careful about the use of film. People tend to feel more comfortable with the flow of continuity in film. They will black out the slides and watch only the screen with the film. However, some creative folk in worship have transposed films over slides (or slides over film). This kind of mix forces the person to use his experience to interrelate the different stimuli.

The switch from color to black and white to negatives really adds to the media show. Endless possibilities crop up before the person working in this electric environment.

How does all of this relate to that particular person? What does this do to Tom? He is being fed the stimuli which turn him on. However, there are two dangers. The medium might wipe out the message. Technique and individual stimuli might erase the message. On the other hand, Tom might stay on an individual trip and become too subjective and inner-directed. Celebration happens on the wings of community. The personal experience must be merged in some actual way with the personhood of others. Every existent medium which has been used or will be used in the future risks this danger. The creative enablers must continually struggle against this kind of temptation. As we have suggested earlier, all of our people come to worship with a media sophistication which is much more highly developed than either you or they realize. The environment has forced them to deal with electric patterns of information retrieval and persuasion. However, we are moving in a tricky area where the celebration of faith is concerned. Tom and others bring expectations and baggage of great variety to our worship services. He may want to come and hide. However, I doubt this. I think that he would come with doubts about himself and the content of this exercise.

Maybe confession and forgiveness would also be important for him. We have suggested elsewhere how this explosive area may be explored. I keep thinking of a former professor who made an unusual gesture when confronted by an alcoholic. The man had killed several people during the war and could not shake the guilt. The professor asked the man to kneel before him. He then placed his hands on his head and told him that he would never commit this sin again and that in the name of Christ he was forgiven of all sin. This moment of being touched and assured of the faith reality changed the man's life. My professor had ritualized acceptance. Perhaps certain ritual expressions could meet the unstable and disjointed

Confession and affirmation

needs of my friend. We have been too timid about creating or assisting the creation of new myths and ritualistic forms. Man creates these extensions of himself and his faith all the time. The myths of John Wayne and Woodstock are as important to some people as the deliverance of the Jewish people from Egypt is to the contemporary Jew. The gunfighter and free spirit are worshiped and their victories are celebrated by a faithful following through the role of mass electric media. If man cannot identify with the gunfighter, football hero, or rock singer he has a problem.

With whom does Tom relate? To whom should he look for patterns of existence? The role of other persons will be the key to his struggle to work out his problems. Being taken seriously as a person is important to everyone. Two men from the phone company spent the day working on my phones. One man told me about a worship experience he had had the previous Sunday. He said that the six members of his family had been camping for the weekend near a little town in Ohio. They scouted out the nearest Catholic Church. As they were entering, they introduced themselves to the priest. The parish is small. The priest called each family present by name to participate in the Mass. At the end he called up the phone man and his family by name! This personal touch really impressed the visiting family. They were invited as persons to partake of the Good News.
With what do we send Tom home? He goes alone into a world that he knows will destroy him if it can. He has no protection of self-confidence or close community. What does the gospel say to my friend who knows that he is crazy, but that the world is still mad? What happens when the worship leaders have not really answered these questions for themselves? What do you enable to take place when you feel as sick and in need as the neediest in the congregation? Perhaps it is at this very juncture that real celebration can happen. I think that it is a much more dangerous situation when the enablers don't confront themselves in such a way to make themselves aware (or willing) to admit their own needs. Worship experiences are not manufactured by superior beings for the simple servants. Worship embraces and reduces everyone to being brothers and sisters in the same mad world with a streak of insanity sweeping through all of us. Such truth is demanded by participants such as Tom. Nothing can happen to him in worship unless we have undergone his pain and suffering in some degree.

"This is Christ's body broken for you, Tom."

"When I use a word it means just what I choose it to mean — neither more nor less...." *

Ken

Ken is also a friend. We have been very close these past couple of years. He has just left for another job in a very different context. He is a colleague who leads worship himself. If he were going to be present at Heinz Chapel when I conduct this worship experience, I would need to become sensitive to a number of important factors.

Ken is the kind of person who reads avidly. Every book on Christian education, theology, science fiction, and anything else which catches his meandering interest is devoured on the spot. He is continually struggling with the interlocked battle of feeling and intellect. His mind keeps grasping for more and more information.

We have talked at length about the interrelationship of the linear and the electric. He is convinced that the Word must be spoken to maintain society and communication. We have not come to the end of our discussion.

However, Ken's presence would suggest that there must be an articulation of the gospel in such a way that people would understand the Word. How is the Word to be spoken and received? This might suggest a flood of responses from a number of contexts. The sermon or homily aspect of the

*Lewis Carroll, *Through the Looking Glass* (New York: Copyright 1965 by Airmont Publishing Co., Inc.), p. 198.

traditional worship service can take many fresh forms. Teams of men can develop authentic dialogue approaches which not only struggle with the spoken word of God between the leaders, but also bring in the random comments of other worshipers.

Drama

The whole realm of the dramatic arts has been missing so far from our ramble through the possibilities of liturgy. Bob Finch has done much to utilize this art form to deliver the Word to the people during worship. He has written plays, used puppets, and employed pantomime to give new forms to the basic substance of the message. He has built dramatic forms to set the stage for communion. If the sacraments are the enacted Word of God, how do we link the articulated word to the sensed manifestation? This question is left unresolved in most contemporary worship which explores new forms. Just doing a play in the sanctuary doesn't assure understanding. However, the Covenant Players and Sandra and Norman Dietz have electrified congregations with their art during worship. They use drama as a connective between the layers of the mind and spirit.

Guerrilla or unexpected drama has been used by a number of so-called "radical Christians." They find that an unexpected intrusion of this kind of fierce drama can open up real worship. This has to be carefully probed. Just walking down the aisle with a rifle on your shoulder doesn't mean that the worshipers are going to understand. Even the follower in the barrel will not assure that the message of peace has been digested by all.

It is distressing to see how many nonliturgical Protestant clergymen depend on the read Word for the presentation of the sacraments. They stand there and have to read the Good News to their people: "this is My body." The Word in this case needs to become flesh. The clergyman doesn't have it in himself yet. How can he expect the people of God to digest it?

Perhaps the people of God should participate in a linear sense as the Word is being verbally expressed. We could give the worshipers an outline and let them follow and make suggestions and notes along the way. This practice would enable them to be part of what is usually one man's thing. The sermon might even be left without an ending. Ask the people to take the pencils that are already in the pews and write an ending from their commitment of faith. These conclusions could be shared at the debriefing afterward or during the service.

Slides for reinforcement

The speaker might even try visual reinforcement of what he is saying. Slides could be dropped in on a screen behind him as he talks. Why not print a collage on the cover of the bulletin? Ask the people to let their eyes move across the collection of pictures to find what visual support they need to participate in what is being said.

In his preaching and teaching Ken is conscious of structure. The reasoning and pace of what he is trying to communicate flows in such a way that you are carried along with it. He can take even the most disagreeable position and make it "reasonable." Our proclamation of the Word must keep these factors in mind if we are to feed into mind and heart. How does one develop the spoken word? So many clergymen are caught in the tight isolated box of lonely preparation of their sermons. John Lennon's rendering of the word "is-o-lation" captures this kind of loneliness.

Some worship leaders have used preparatory discussion groups as background for a particular sermon. These groups have included nonbelievers who have been hostile to the church. There have been rare team ministries where two men have worked together in the preparation of the preached word. They either preach to each other or perhaps both preach on the same text after preparing and sharing it together. Each man would take a different service without announcing who would preach which time in order to keep competition out of it.

From crowd to cadre

As I have suggested elsewhere, the spoken word fits best where there can be a response by the people. Peter preached at Pentecost and the people went into small groups and celebrated the faith together. Perhaps the ushers should carry in the elements of a love feast (rolls and coffee?) and set them at the worship center as the service concludes. The people can immediately come together and share their insights into the Word of God. Ken has another streak of personhood which is important to our probing for a service to meet people's needs. He is deeply interested in the world of the mystical reaches of the mind. This expresses itself in his interest in science fiction and studies of psychic phenomena. We must build in some appreciation for the spiritual power of worship. Too often the main religious traditions have failed to be faithful to the spiritual aspect of their history. They have forced their people who have spiritual sensitivity to form sects. The power and mystery of the worship celebration is a major part of the history of the mainline faith. How do we faithfully allow such manifestations to be represented? It is so easy to treat such spiritual interests as fads. The authentic manifestation of the Holy Spirit is separated from the misuse of excitement by a very fine line.

Ken's interest should remind us to permit the spiritual sensitivity of our people to find form and expression. These enabling dimensions to worship are difficult to create. Worship leaders tend to fill in all the spaces in the worship structure. There is no room for something to happen among the people. What would happen if the Holy Spirit were indeed present and called his people to new life? Most leaders would hope that he would use the order of worship to do it. A few years ago we visited a Reform temple to experience a Seder celebration. At one point in the event the door was opened to invite the prophet to return and take his place at the empty place. We were told that this is a moment of expectation. However, as we celebrated that moment, the door was opened and shut immediately. The person in charge of that task really didn't believe that the missing guest would return! The same kind of loss of faith is revealed when Christians gather around their sacraments. There are differing interpretations of just what happens in the communion or Mass event. However, the mind-set evident in those coming and leaving the celebration suggests that they no longer really believe that they are going to experience the meaning of it in their lives. It is good to participate in the sacraments. However, I am not really different after having participated in this mystery.

Ken's particular interests and the general growth of cultism suggest to me that the religious community had better look into itself about the care of its mysteries. Why is it that the sacramental interest in Protestantism has been lacking until very recently? It was important at the beginning of the Reformation. How do we celebrate this mystery in the contemporary situation?

Passing the loaf

There are a number of exciting probes going on concerning sacramental celebrations. In the Protestant circles a variety of material substances have been used to celebrate communion. The practice of passing a loaf and having each person break off a piece is quite common. This return to a real loaf of bread has been an attempt to enable the worshiper to feel the reality of this act. The commonness of the loaf as the element of communion came to mind a number of years ago when I was participating in a communion service conducted by Marshal L. Scott. We had been working in the Presbyterian Institute of Industrial Relations for the summer. The service was bringing to a conclusion our three months of work as laborers and factory workers. Our evenings had been spent in seminars concerning the implications of the Christian faith on our real work experiences among real working folk. The service was delayed. Apparently a hungry man had come off the street and stolen the loaf on the communion table. He had taken it to feed himself! On one retreat we used hamburger buns as the common substance we had. Stories are told about the use of soft drinks for the blood of Christ. Many worshipers have used the process of dipping the bread into the wine or juice.

Jacinta has reminded us that we will have people from different backgrounds present for the summer service I am planning. This means that actual sacraments cannot be part of our celebration. It is important for us to remember that most Protestant congregations are really a mixture of backgrounds. We may have great confidence in our membership training classes. (Do they exist in most local situations?) However, a lot of people really worship the way they have been taught in the past and not at all the way the clergyman assumes. This means that expectations and responses may be hard to read when something like the sacraments is celebrated.

New rituals

A lot of creative people are creating mini-sacramental rituals for the worship celebration. They are drawing upon the element of mystery and the power of the Spirit to provide something meaningful and fresh. The love feast is a good example of this kind of event. It is not nailed down to the sacramental tradition, nor is it governed by the restrictions of the other main sacraments in most traditions. However, it is pretty clear that the church in the earliest times had these kinds of table celebrations. Some communities have used these table celebrations as a means of getting Christians from different traditions together as worshiping brothers and sisters.

I have often used this style of worship as part of learning events. This works particularly well when we have been through an all-day game event. There is a closeness and excitement that can be the context to enable worship to really happen. We often set the tables around in a circle. There may be a loaf in the middle of the circle. We sometimes build in the traditional aspects of worship (confession, thanksgiving, intercession, petition, etc.). We always close such experiences with a sharing of touch or with embraces.

Again, I have to keep coming back to the givens before me. There will be a large group of people. I can't do many of the things that small groups can best do. The size of the group is a key factor in planning. Certain goals are impossible to accomplish in certain contexts. It is best to establish the thrust of what is to be sought so that there won't be frustration when some of the mixed objectives are unfulfilled. Yet, it is helpful to let the flow of ideas run in and out of our minds when we are enabling creative liturgy to happen. Words do not always say what we want to mean. We cannot always control what people are going to do with them either.

Your mind is the screen

Roy

When Roy first walked into my office I knew that he was an artist. He was looking for a job. He hoped to become a film editor for a local television station. He got the job. He chain-smoked throughout our time together. He was tense and anxious. He showed me one of the films he had just finished. It was good. He had imagination and lots of film experience. However, Pittsburgh is a lousy place to raise money for these kinds of film projects.

Roy and I talked a lot. I guess it was disappointing for him to accept the fact that I had no bread for his project. I tried to work out something whereby he could do some background film work for a television show I was developing for CBS. Through this avenue of sharing I found that he had also been on "Look Up and Live" a few years ago. At that time he appeared as a singer. He had been one of the first people to sing Bob Dylan's "Times Are A-Changin'" on national television. Again our discussion came to a dead end for him. The producer at CBS didn't want to follow my initial ideas on the use of film. He went for an outdoor setting and finally did the show in a church camp in New Jersey.

Roy and I see each other occasionally when I visit the station where he works. He is doing quite well. I do know that he has recorded an album of his songs for private distribution. I like them.

Roy represents a combination of factors concerning the celebration I am planning for the University chapel. I know that he would dig the possible media dimensions of the service. He would appreciate the electric medium if it were well done. He would be distracted by sloppy craftsmanship. This is an important factor. So many times we have worshipers who have individual skills which are highly developed. Do they sit back and respond critically to the way the service functions in their areas of expertise? I know that I have a hard time not falling into this kind of spectator trap. We might be quite surprised to know the real craftsmanship of our worshipers. We have such poor guideposts to who our people are that we do not often tap these skills. We ask a banker to take the offering. We don't know how turned on he is by photography or music.

Roy will not only critically look at the media we happen to use. He may also find himself framing the thrust of the action as if it were a film. This is an interesting exercise. Corita Kent and others have trained students to see the portions of visual perspective in order to grasp the whole flow of continuity. She will send them into a garbage dump or used car lot with a small card. The card has one square hole in it. They spend several hours just discovering the bits and pieces in order to put the large tapestry of life together. Roy will see the individual frames. He will mentally edit out moments of flaw. These points when action is disturbed and the content lost will be plucked out by the editor in his mind. How can fluidity and informality be structured so as not to let it get in the way of freedom? Those churches where the ushers click their heels after they have carefully placed you in the proper seat are just too much. However, there is a natural flow which makes the moments along the way seem a part of one swell of faith.

Roy's intensity suggests to me that I must be continually aware throughout this planning process to keep the emotional needs of the worshiper in mind. I am not called to cause pain and discomfort just for the sake of it. Roy likes the fresh and meaningful. However, he doesn't want to be placed on the spot or be made to look foolish. The world of electric media seduces us into desiring more experience and involvement. At the same time, it makes us incredibly aware of ourselves and other people's judgment upon us. We are longing for personal involvement while at the same time afraid to be placed in an awkward position. This duality is played upon extensively in the advertising game. We are promised that a product will make us the talk of the neighborhood because of the shiny floor it gives us. This approval is underscored by the opening scene of an ad where the bridge group makes fun of a lady because she used the old waxing product. Approval is so much better than ridicule.

My film editor friend is also used to an environment where he has control. I was visiting him at the station one day. He was editing film for the 6:00 P.M. news. I remarked that he seemed to edit the film footage at will. He said that he alone usually decides on what will be used and what will be left upon the cutting room floor. What power. The visual support of a news story for television will be decided by Roy. The scenes one views as a story is read will make all the difference in the world to the viewer. Just mismatch a sound track to some slides. It will make the sound seem ironic.

People come to worship and desire to have as much or more mastery of the situation than they have in life. I discussed earlier how people search for comfort or nostalgia which is very controllable. When we start to experiment with liturgy, we rob them of this mastery. They don't know what will happen next. We often reduce the worshiper to a helpless position. This can be very unproductive. Roy will want to feel that he comes before God as one who can give and exercise his responsibility and freedom. The work context of a worshiper's life does have a bearing on the celebration event. He brings a lot of vocational baggage that we often ignore. Some worshipers have much guilt over what they must do to earn their income. They may hate the work or know that it is basically useless or dishonest. Roy is excited about his work. However, our probe of him makes me aware of the role work may play in structuring a worship event.

Music

My friend is also into music. We have plowed through many rambling thoughts about music. However, we may get some data from the kind of music he likes. This information is not enough in itself. We may be tempted to generalize from the kind of music he particularly enjoys. However, it is even better to search with him about the music. It is most important to know what he likes about the music he likes. He may like it for an entirely different reason than does another person. It is significant that he projects himself into it. I am lucky to have explored this dimension of his interest with him. Roy writes and plays music. It is what one might label "folk music." There is a gentleness about it. He told me that he wrote only one protest song. Such a brief exploration of his music world suggests that I might use contemporary message songs if they are real vehicles of a message. He would find singing to be a valid means of expressing his faith in a corporate setting. This is his gift.

Roy gives me some important insights into the kinds of things I must consider if he were to be there. He forces me to realize that the individual is a mini-receiver. He takes the elements of the event into himself. The screen for this translation is the mind. His mind tells me a lot about the celebration we are creating.

Got any spare change, mister?

Last night Bob and I went to the kind of celebration he enjoys the most. The response to this community opportunity was amazing. Eighteen thousand people crowded into the large arena. The community was quite faithful in supporting this expression of faith. They had paid out anywhere from $4.50 to $6.50 for this one event. The expectation was impressive. You could just feel the tension in the air. The unimportant fringe rites familiar to everyone who has ever attended a religious celebration were endured. The early music was just a filler for the big attraction.

The moment for the Word to become reality was about to break forth. As the bearer of this crowd's expectation prepared to make the proclamation, everyone was alert and ready to break loose. Suddenly it happened! The focus of celebration was there! In an electric flash the enabler of this hope and his brethren were beginning—the Rolling Stones in person!

The Stones

It is hard to describe moments like this. The message and the medium are in your head. You have heard their songs for so long. Then you have them there to massage you in the flesh—Mick and his folk. They are so together. The eighteen thousand faithful are pounding out a response. In fact, on one of the pirated versions (illegally recorded albums) of the concert which appeared later you couldn't hear the Stones' rhythm section. You could, however, hear how the audience provided the human beat of feet, hands, and voices to drive them on. It is interesting to note that back in the early days of the religious tradition (almost any faith tradition) there used to be pirated versions of the Scripture and worship rites. Now we have pirated versions of the demigods from the rock world.

It may seem a strain of analogy to compare a music celebration to a worship service. However, the points of intersection between the two thrusts of human interest are striking. At the concert attended by Bob and me there was even a sacramental aspect. The people immediately in front of us lighted up a hash pipe and freely shared the drug with brothers and sisters around them. The communicant would slowly take a drag and let the smoke carefully escape from his lungs. There was a look of contentment and acceptance among the folk who were smoking and taking in the sounds together. Jumpin' Jack Flash himself was before them. The recital of the music repeated so often on home sound gear was now being manifested in the midst of those who believed and celebrated. Familiarity was the main feature of what was happening. The gathered celebrants wanted it to be the way they imagined that it would be.

The audience was responsive. They kept swelling toward the front. They wanted to touch Mick as he teasingly danced before them. The Altamont experience with the Stones suggests that pop-deity also has demonic dimensions. The fact that people can be driven to ecstasy of hatred and love by the kind of pop celebration we were attending is worth our consideration. There are numerous examples of religious celebrations which cause great emotional reaction on the part of the worshipers. "Revivals" still are aimed at getting the gathered to make ecstatic responses to the appeal of the message. However, it seems that football games and musical events are the only consistent celebrations which get this kind of response in our day. There are many stories and personal experiences which come to me at this moment concerning the care and love such musical events enable to be expressed.

The church's attempt to do its truth as worship is different from this evening in the Civic Arena. However, it is important for me to plan my chapel event with the kinds of clues this pop celebration suggests. We actually tried to build upon these insights last summer. Why hadn't someone thought of it before? A rock festival is a new expression of celebration and a way for high school young people to explore the meaning of Christ for their lives.

"Dawn"

The idea of this Christian rock festival-celebration came to a group of ministers from a cluster of United Presbyterian churches in Pittsburgh, as they struggled with the problem of developing a relevant and meaningful program for high school young people.

The usual rally to be held in a local high school auditorium first came to mind. Then one of the ministers asked, "Have you seen the film *Woodstock?* It seems to me that this forces us to approach the idea of gathering a community of young people in a totally different way."

"I saw love and affirmation coming from the stage at all times," answered another minister who had seen the film. "It was like a credo which became reality. Nobody bad-rapped anyone else. The people at Woodstock lived up to what was being proclaimed."

"What hit me about the film," answered another, "was the freedom of activity which swirled around the tribal drum from the stage at Woodstock. People could choose what they wanted to do."

The genesis of Pittsburgh's Christian folk-rock festival titled, "Dawn: The Beginning of a Personal Odyssey," came from this conversation. Odyssey here referred to the journey every Christian takes with Christ.

Young people and adults from thirty churches planned and brought the festival to life. The time was a beautiful Sunday afternoon from 1:00 to 7:00. The site was the Allegheny County Fairgrounds. The participants were five thousand young people from a nine-county area.

The "program" included an endless stream of musicians who played on a central stage or did small intimate "turns" in one of the nearby buildings. The festival's depth and bite rested largely on the caliber of the talent. The musicians were relevant, committed, and skilled. John Rydgren, Lutheran minister and former anchorman for the ABC FM network, was host for the day. Electric musicians such as House of Tito Luv, John Guest and the Exkursions, Salt and Pepper, and the Blues Condition filled the air with rock vibes. Folk music writer-performers Mel Reisz, Mose Henry, Gorman and Clark, Barb Ray, and Father John Dee also rapped and played.

This rock festival and celebration, as might be expected, came under some fire from city and county officials as plans developed and were made known. Several park permits for rock festivals planned by local radio stations were cancelled at the last minute. But when park officials reviewed the plans for "Dawn," they permitted the festival to continue. However, tickets (at one dollar) had to be sold in advance—at churches in the area. This meant that people apart from church groups were not encouraged to drop in. And the advertising had to bear the religious emphasis of the event, which discouraged the general public from coming. This narrowed the original idea of a broader outreach for the festival.

The day of "Dawn" was bright and clear, even so. The one hundred "marshals," who had been prepared ahead of time at a series of training events, provided support for the entertainers or mixed to give the event cohesiveness.

The starting time of 1:00 P.M. was close to church dismissals and made a lot of the people late. But the crowd kept growing, since the design for the festival made it easy to enter into the happening whenever people came.

The six and a half hours of music and love were enjoyed from every vantage point. One crowd of people gathered before the stage to dig the sounds from the center stage. Others wandered from barn to barn to take in the rap sessions and mini-concerts with the groups not currently on stage. Some of these sessions broke into instant workshops. Gorman and Clark, for example, rapped about their experimentation in Chicago with music and liturgy, and a group of high school students interested in introducing this kind of thing into their church pushed toward me.

Father John Dee, after completing his stage performance, let a crowd of seventy-five experience a mix of secular and sacred sounds and sights. He flashed slides on the side of the barn wall and sang.

Five hundred high school students in the Agriculture Building expressed their approval with applause, shouts, and the stomping of feet, as the Exkursions played their heavy rock and sang, "Give Christ a Chance." Mime Dan Kamin let his body express man's quest for understanding, while later his lips articulated his concern for peace as he talked with twenty-five students.

As tired Festival director David Hall stood beside the stage, a couple of barefooted, barebacked students moved up beside him. Their faces and backs were burned from the afternoon sun. "Hey, thanks for the day. It was really something else." Dave smiled and the students moved on.

During the special folk celebration which concluded the day, a county policeman said quietly as he watched the mass of people worshiping: "I guess we were too worried about this event." He looked over the cars, vans, and mounted police. "We have had no trouble at all. It was a very good day."

Such a Christian rock festival is not a prescription for future youth events. It is not a program which should be used by everyone. "Dawn" was simply an exploration into what can happen when adults and young people try to do something real and authentic together in the name of Christ. It was a good day, and for many it was the beginning of or at least the way station on a personal odyssey with Jesus Christ. How do you move from a real rock concert or a special Christian outdoor event to the confines of a chapel? How are these good vibes captured in the kind of worship we must do? How can I translate the lump in my throat as I experienced the reality of pop heroes into a language of faith? The presence of the Holy Spirit should also be a moment of excitement and expectation. If Mick Jagger blows my mind, what should Christ be doing to all of us in celebration?

Mick or Jesus?

When I posed these questions to a friend of mine, his answer was quite direct. "Have Mick do the worship service." He was being more than funny with that suggestion. There are a number of rock groups doing the religious circuit. Why is it that I feel uncomfortable about this approach? Maybe I suspect that the people who were reviving people two years ago in blue suits and short haircuts have now just changed uniforms as a gimmick. I guess that I am caught in my own trap. I have been dipping into the life-styles and mind-sets of people in search of the shape and skin of worship. However, so many of the attempts to develop a whole system of religious communication around one facet of the cultural forms seems limited. Perhaps Christian rock (if there is such a thing) is great on the one-day event or at the retreat. Yet, forms can never be static and remain as true vessels of the living faith message.

Russell Block

I guess that I am raising these questions for myself because I just finished listening once again to a tape sent to me by innovative teaching pastor Russell Block. He is a man turned on by the whole world of art. In his case, we can say the whole world and mean it. In the course of six years with one people, he has taken them through every imaginable form of art as media for worship (drama, dance, pop-rock-jazz-classical original music, locally and commercially produced films, puppetry, banner, etc.). This is a local setting with lots of people who don't dig this kind of thing. Yet, through Russell's goodwill and inclusive spirit they continue to do worship in this innovative way. He is not riding a personal hobbyhorse or a fad. He moves through the planning in a very orderly fashion. The committee on innovative worship studies the standards of worship, goes into New York for personal experiences of new forms of expression, and draws upon community talent. Russell's approach seems so much more authentic than what any of us do in these one-night stands!

I can't put down the idea that Mick Jagger could do a good worship experience. Who knows? I hear that the music event in memory of the late Stone, Brian, was very moving and worshipful in a rock manner. Who can judge? I do know that the Stones' concert turned Bob and me on. So many times in worship I don't get turned on by God! Wow! This is the kind of crunch a lot of us may be experiencing.

Al Johnson's tape has just passed through my head. He expresses my grasping for perspective about this question in another way. He claims that he and his folk got turned on by a mountain worship service. The appeal of the rural service he describes as being serendipity ("the ability to find unexpected delights everywhere"). Al criticizes his own worship leadership as being too structured and predictable. However, loose, spirit-led services tend to lack a direction and satisfaction. He is caught admiring predictability and serendipity! How do we keep a foot in each place without falling on our faces? Whenever I must think through this kind of dilemma, I get the lingering suspicion that we are trapped by our experience and are not free. Perhaps we have limitations of thinking imposed upon us by our past experience. We have been taught to be structured or loose in worship. Perhaps these options are a false separation of the Spirit. Why can't we have Mick and his kind of celebration while at the same time getting into a style of real celebration that lets us go somewhere? We are so tempted by our environment to make these kinds of bad choices. The electric environment calls us to the new life-style or intermix. Facets of celebration are no longer clearly separated. We retreat into compartmentalizing out of fear.

Al Johnson

Bob

Bob is telling me that I must be aware of these factors if he is part of our celebrating people. I must also keep before me the interesting blurs in Bob's mind-set and life-style. He lives with the freaks and the slicks. His community is blue-collar and uptight with "long hairs." The Catholic school he attends is prone to a "hairy necks" approach to the issues of the day. "If they would let us in there with H bombs, we would get the war over." "If a person refuses to go to the service, he should be shot. I don't care if it was my brother. He should be shot."

Out of this tight social cradle Bob has emerged as a free social activist. He works on an underground newspaper and is very political within the movement. He is an artist and very interested in mass media. While he does the heavy scene with the kids at the paper, he also delivers the most conservative newspaper in town as a paper boy!

Bob's religion must take flesh in the lives of people doing something. He doesn't go for words that mask a lack of commitment. He wants the world to be changed. There are so many revolutionary things about worship celebration! If we accept the radical change that comes to human life when Jesus Christ becomes the Word of human life, then worship becomes the celebration of this fact. Perhaps the form of this content should be felt more often in worship. Bob would appreciate a sensitivity to human need in the worship service we are planning. Do I dip into the prophets for this kind of mentality? What kind of Jesus should be shared if we pay particular attention to the passages reflecting Jesus' rebuke of those who have fallen short of his call for a new life?

Creative or innovative liturgy is quite dangerous for some. It is very tempting for the artist or poetic spirit to miss the bite and drive of the religious tradition which calls man to combat his selfish self and care for others. Once a group of worshiping people get trapped into an artistic bag they can use this as a cover for reality. Yesterday's form of nostalgia takes new shape with the blessing of the arts. This community of celebration built around the senses and spirit can become more insular than did the straight forms of most traditional worship.

Bob and a host of friends keep reminding me that good liturgy pushes you inside out. We confront God in the context of our brothers and sisters only to discover that the family of man is our responsibility. Creative spirit and sister Doris Schwerin gave us words to express the sorrow of Kent State which every child of God felt. Her litany of despair, hope, and love grew out of good theology and celebration. A subtle network of five hundred persons and churches used this liturgical form to confront their world of pain and hatred with love through worship.

How do you provide order with all these leaves swirling in the air at once? Liturgy isn't an occasion to do politics. God doesn't belong to a particular political party (even if your favorite candidate claims otherwise). The celebration of worship isn't an esoteric orgy of aesthetics. On the other hand, it is all of these things! The folk on the coast have long celebrated the great political crises of our society in a religious context. The Free Church of Berkeley, the Submarine Church, and other brothers and sisters who have made a radical commitment to a Christ that is flesh, celebrate in the streets and fields. Tear gas, occasional rifle shots, and confusion have been the worship context for some of the churches in every age. Troops have worshiped at the intersections of life and death at every given moment someplace.

Ann & Steve

I have worshiped with dying brothers and sisters at hospital bedsides and rest homes. There is nothing new about Bob's need to meet life and human need in worship. Some may say that authentic art captures the heartbeat of life. One cannot go to the world of the arts to escape anything. Art cuts us to the quick. We meet ourselves and something a bit beyond our grasp listening to a song by Ann Lawrence or confronting the puppets of Steve Brezzo.

Back to the chapel! Back to August! How do I pull all of Bob's contributions of personhood into my task? I could use many of the artistic resources of Pittsburgh. Perhaps I could use some of Bob's art! I could blow up portions of his line drawings on slides. We could intermix the music, social concerns, and art of this teen-ager as part of the celebration event. The idea of the worshipers bringing gifts of sharing for the celebration is always intriguing. Duane Holm has been creative in facilitating liturgy as an actualization of the theological thrust of his people. The Community of Reconciliation worships by having each family bring a slice of bread for the elements of the Lord's Supper. One family brings the wine. The common bread rises from the common folk.

When the Stones played for us, the sacramental use of dope was shocking for some from outside the rock community who were present. The churchman should be particularly concerned. He has been given the responsibility of making the body and blood of Christ the feast of thanksgiving. In his hands the bread should rise. However, the celebration of this sacrament within Protestant circles is disgraceful. There is no rising bread and flowing blood of life for the folk who sup only three or four times a year. The churchman guards the treasure chest while people sup elsewhere. God will not be denied. The folk must be fed.

It is particularly hard to discover that substitute sacraments (dope, etc.) are being used by hungry people. We rot the body. We defile the blood. We squeeze the validity out of the means of grace and then act scandalized by the fruits of what we have created.

> Hungry people drop out of the fellowship where they are left wanting.
>
> Hungry people scour the alleys and garbage dumps to feed on anything.
>
> Hungry people devour one another in pettiness and hostility.
>
> Hungry people fall into boredom and sleep when they should fight for survival.
>
> Hungry people die.

Thank you, God, for Daddy's birthday and the celebration

Today was my birthday. It was an exciting day. As I write this, I am very happy. A strange kind of euphoria fills me. I can't really put my finger on

76

Happy Birthday, D.C.B.!

the reasons behind this good feeling. Maybe I am just coming down after so much pressure from the past four years.

I think that this day of celebration with my family is a better explanation. Amy and Jill love celebrations. For two little (two and a half and five and a half) girls, it seems that life is to enjoy and celebrate. At this time so many things seem to fit into this happy life. There is a place for puppies, Dairy Queens, Mother, drawing with a felt-tipped pen, going to the park, God, treats in general, and Dad (often just Dennis). It is all mixed up in a crazy, exciting way. I know that it is a bore to see someone else tripping on love for his wife and children. However, if Amy were present at the Heinz Chapel event what would I have to consider? What would she need, give, or celebrate?

It is hard to take her to worship in most settings. We have to sit a great deal. She and other children who happen into worship with their families must spend the time drawing on bulletin covers (That's what they are for!). They have to tame their restless bodies to be proper for most Protestant worship. I guess that we assume that the adult has the body in total control (numb). The grown-up uses his head for worship.

Amy would like the body movement that turned on my friend John. She would dig his interest in dancing and touch. Jill is even more into a touch trip. She must test everything with her fingers or tongue. At two and a half you are not very sophisticated. We are told by the cultural tracking pattern that she is not yet fully developed. When she is trained to know better, she will not explore her world in this way. She will scan each new confrontation intellectually and make judgments on the basis of this limited data.

Amy and Jill have been disappointed when they have stayed in the worship experiences designed for adults. They just aren't like the kinds of celebrations they design themselves.

Take my birthday party today. Amy and Jill really had input for it. They worked much of the day on the big event for the four of us. Daddy worked on that book. They kept coming down with delightful grins which indicated that they knew about something quite wonderful that was going to happen to me. Jill couldn't keep it together as a secret. She wandered in at one point with her party hat on and started talking with excitement about what was going to happen.

Singing was very much a part of their celebration pattern. I got the "happy birthday" song several times during our meal and cake. Each had to kiss me and give me the presents she had made. Amy had taken a paper cup and decorated it with crayon drawings, Scotch tape, and scrap paper. An American Bible Society "Love" stamp was featured in the artwork. It was not one of her representative pictures. She volunteered the fact that this drawing was a "design."

We feasted on chicken and then . . . cake and ice cream. Amy was quite particular how she wanted it. "Chocolate or vanilla, but no strawberry." She wanted to know how old I was. This discussion developed into a discussion of people dying. Soon we were talking about Jesus. "Can I sit on his lap?"

In these few comments about a typical family celebration we find so many of the key elements of liturgical celebration! The place of ritual, love, hope, death, and community are part of my daughters' lives. They are as set about certain elements of worship celebration as are the most conservative adults. At the same time, they reinforce a number of the hunches we have gleaned from our potential congregation.

The day hasn't been all joy and love. Amy kicked herself and we had blood and tears. I took her into the house. She had cut herself at the same place two days ago. The fresh wound caused a stream of blood. She was very frightened. She didn't want her sock removed from her foot. Amy was sure that it would hurt. I told her to trust me to be careful. I removed the sock swiftly in order to reduce the pain from friction. She was tearfully frightened about having the bandage put on the wound. I told her that she could trust me. I put it on with minimal pain. "You have hands of healing, Daddy." What a strange, beautiful way to respond to a mini-crisis in her life!

Amy's experience and response raise the whole role of the caring understructure of a celebrating people. I remember a Saturday night spent with an elder's husband. Her husband suddenly lost control of himself. He kept crying and crying. He became hysterical. We rushed him to the hospital. He was committed to the unit for mental patients. Nothing would be known about his condition for a week or so. (The next morning Ann would be present for the worship service.) I returned home at 3:00 A.M. It

Celebration of life and a discussion of death

Daddy heals

was suddenly clear that I could not preach on the text prepared. The focus of the gospel now reflects the needs of this family. Their pain and suffering is the focus of our concern as a gathered people. We had communion often in that church. The next morning the Word spoken and enacted was made manifest on the occasion of this family's need. What energy and power were present that morning!

Every good clergyman enters the realm of celebration with this kind of understructure. He has suffered with his people. He has struggled with them as they try to confess and receive forgiveness. Yet, what does he do with this kind of communion that is present in the congregational body? There are always present these kinds of experiential threads which hold together a people in the deepest ways possible. How can these threads be gently tugged to enable the people to cuddle together as one people? How can the experience of suffering together provide new roads of communication never possible before the sharing of suffering?

"Rap Around"

Power and unity are in the brotherhood of those who have suffered together. At least, there can be such communion if a person of faith utilizes the opportunity such experiences give. Each week I do a live radio show on the local rock station (KQV ABC Pittsburgh). "Rap Around" is conducted differently from most talk shows. There is no hassle in our kind of communication. We are tribes gathered electronically to celebrate life as persons. Most of the calls from youth and young adults are about personal problems. The mail each week is staggering. Ratings suggest that three-fourths of the teen-agers interviewed listen to "Rap Around." The strange thing about this public sharing of suffering and difficulty is that it creates a real basis of understanding and trust. I will walk into a group of people. Once it is learned that I am the guy who does "Rap Around" we are immediately into a heavy rap. The medium of radio has created a means of communication that is carried over into other kinds of relationships. So it is in worship. Good worship can be facilitated by a rich life together as a people. Good worship can facilitate a rich life together as a people. It works in both directions.

To crying Amy, I have hands of healing. To a loving, caring people there is a foundation upon which the healing of God's love can be found. Authentic worship must always build upon such shared experience. In a sense, worship is the celebration of what has happened, is happening, and will happen. This strain of thought is touching once again my concern for the role of history. My fathers and brothers in faith—the Jews—have most faithfully preserved this important heritage for me. They still remember how God delivered them out of slavery and brought them into freedom. The Christian too easily forgets his reasons for celebration.

Amy is suggesting to me that celebration must also embrace death. How alien this is to the American way of living. Yet, the finality of our life experience is acknowledged each time we worship. The substructure of destruction and final death is ever present when we celebrate the life, death, and resurrection of Jesus Christ and all the saints who now sleep. In most worship services, death is barely mentioned in passing. The actual worship at the funeral is either a celebration of worldly values and success, or escapism about the "next life."

My church sacraments professor shared with us his staggering experience of entering a funeral home to conduct a service for an unknown man who had died without relatives or friends. The funeral director apologized because he couldn't be present for the service. Dr. Lower thought that this was a strange thing to mention. He entered the chapel area to find that no one was present except the dead man! He started the service without a living soul. His mind raced over what he was doing. Why was he doing this service? Only the deceased was present. Was the service for the living or the dead? Where were the people of God at this time of celebration?

Death is really celebrated

There are exceptions to this kind of empty ritual. For example, when Paul Younger died prematurely in a car accident, the black worship outlook took over. There was a celebration at that service! The people had an opportunity to acknowledge the loss of their brother. They also marched out of the church to demonstrate their concern for a social problem as part of the service! By this action they were saying that the death of one brother can result in the resurrection of active love for the rest of God's people.

Amy's life touches death as must every life. How do we enable her to join the dance of celebration which must be part of life itself? The awesome conclusion to *The Seventh Seal* flashes before me. Death and his victims (Or was it comrades?) moving across the horizon was grim yet satisfying.

The older nurseryman stands quite stiffly before the church study group as he gives his presentation on the life and death of the earth. His weathered body bears witness to his lifelong struggle to protect the earth and the abused people upon it. Only when he starts to describe the way one can nurture a tree into life, does he really sparkle. We are all caught in the magical web of new life and possibility. He suddenly catches our awe about life and gently makes us confront death. "The good earth gives us endless life. Into it we must return. This fact is not without dignity." It seems that if man could see nature as an extension or reflection of man's condition, there would be a great deal more concern with ecology and human life. Amy asks about how and why people die. The answers to her questions are available in man's relationship to his environment. This theological quest is more than the equal responsibility passages of the Old Testament. There is a rhythm and hope in our life.

The church has sometimes acknowledged the kinship between man and his cradle of life. Many of the seasons of the liturgical year were tied to nature at some early point in history. The fact of this relationship is often related to the discussion of how the Judeo-Christian tradition has "recycled" existent seasonal agricultural holidays for its own use. Such a focus concerning only the common process of cultural and theological assimilation misses the point of liturgical power. Perhaps it is a strange denial of the basic human process that has forced us into the "stuffed doll" approach to celebration. There is a relationship between the baggage we bring to worship and the nature of the content of the service. Amy and other untrained spirits keep forcing us to get down to the basics. There can be no soaring without taking off from some base of reality.

How to die and be buried

The celebration of life and death can be good worship and good living. From the simple life of the Trappists at Gethsemane, Kentucky, Father Matthew Kelty tells of the monks' way of celebrating death. The body is washed and watched over by the brothers who read the Psalms. After a morning funeral Mass, the body is set to rest deep in the Kentucky earth. "The body is treated with reverence and love, but is not embalmed or falsified in any way. Nor do we use a casket or box, since the Brother is being returned to the mother which bore him and who will keep him in her depths until the last day." The beauty of this account is striking. It is even more arresting because of the publication for which Father Kelty wrote:

Whole Earth Catalog (July 1970, p. 37). This is the amazing sourcebook of living close to nature produced by a commune in California. The subculture finds meaning and beauty in the simplicity of good celebration.

Another aspect of Amy's becoming character is her delight in the unexpected. She has her rituals. However, she also relishes the possibility of the impossible. It is thrilling to spring something joyous on her. "Let's go to the amusement place." Her eyes sparkle. She is transfixed with the idea of what will be coming now. Any worship experience for Amy will have to contain the unexpected. What surprises can happen in worship? The order of worship printed in the bulletin robs us of any unexpected events. Russell Block, who has done a great deal in innovative worship prepares his people at the beginning of the service for what is going to happen. However, we are generally caught in liturgical settings where only the sermon or spoken message may contain some surprises. What about the content of our message itself? What is there within the message itself that should reach out and confront us with the new and unexpected? These are questions of indictment for those celebrating in most contexts.

Amy is a pretty good judge of authenticity. If I turn her on with expectation and then just let her down, she is disappointed and more critical next time. This is why the ingredients of freedom and expectation are so hard to program. We cannot put people on by using some gimmick. We also shouldn't promise more than we can deliver. This kind of "forced" high can often be felt when a worship leader is trapped by his own reputation. The unresponsive congregation can just feel the escalation as he pulls out all the stops (tricks). He must get them to respond. This is why he has been invited as the "revival" speaker.

Our people deserve and demand more. The content of the Good News promises more. How do we prepare the vehicles (ourselves) in order that such promise and expectation may be fulfilled? The children and adults pose this challenge to us by their presence as people responding to the calling of Christ's promise.

The merry-go-round really does something to Amy. She gets such a kick out of the endless movement. She is thrilled by the strange things that this whirling experience does to her body. Her head swims with dizziness. The rest of her body is extremely sensitive because of the rushing blood

When you're hot, you're hot!

which has been circulating at an increased pace. The visual sweep of her world is blurred and delightfully distorted. She sometimes just lets her body be carried along with the up and down, whirling motion of the merry-go-round with her head thrown back. How could the service at Heinz Chapel draw some insights from her experience at the amusement concession in the shopping center? Amy knows that there are only so many tickets for rides. She has to make decisions before she commits herself to a particular ride. She chooses what will be most important for her. Then she tries to milk every drop of enjoyment and meaning out of it.

In our summer chapel event I will have to make the offering a meaningful experience for her. She will have to have a sense of making a commitment to something that will be important. The little envelopes will not do it. Maybe she will have to be encouraged to make some other offering of herself. She proudly gives the amusement man her own ticket. She has freely chosen what will be meaningful to her.

It is hard to get her to leave the amusement center behind. There are good memories. However, she knows that the next stop will be for soft pretzels and frozen Coke. She can, in a sense, leave behind her high because the rest of the world will give other highs. Good worship has similiar appeals. After a people has communed in the presence of God and found wholeness and love, it is hard to go back into hostility and uncertainty. However, good worship celebration is that which brings the world along with it. Daily reality in the midst of confusion must be there along with the ageless hope. This means that there will be stops along the way during the week which will be good also. Facets of the familiar will now be parts of something unique and flawless. Merry-go-round and frozen Coke can make a lot of other things bearable.

Amy will not be at the service. I know that I am pushing myself to think that I can really include her in the worshiping household of God as it now stands. I can't defend that statement if I use my understanding of the faith and its celebration. However, this is the way it is in our time.

Just before that birthday celebration for Daddy, Amy led us in prayer. "Thank you, God, for Daddy's birthday and the celebration." Yes, thank you, God and Amy.

That's my gig

Fred

I don't remember how we met. It was several years ago. Fred is a Reform rabbi in a large congregation. It is hard to explain it. We sure make it together as friends and media freaks. We have been in the same room only about six or seven times. He is living in an overloaded environment. I guess we both immediately sensed that we are the kind of guys that speed on media. We both feel the same pressures and the same temptations to do everything that comes our way.

Fred is heavily into the education, coffee house, music, and liturgy bag. He is a musician who can really get it on. The media trip is more than gimmickery for him. He wants to do media with his folk in such a way that they confront themselves, others, and their faith. Fortunately he works within a context which permits him the room he needs to experiment.

Fred is really a brother. Just a few weeks ago we locked ourselves into a room for five hours and just about destroyed each other with ideas. It's the kind of communication which I don't have with too many people. Things don't have to be completely explained. Sentences remain unfinished. He knows what is in my head. I know where he is going once he hints his direction of thought.

"Is Jesus Christ Superstar really a Jewish musical?"

I guess that this kind of communication is different from what generally happens between clergymen. We support each other. I am knocked out by his probes. He is ecstatic about something that worked for me. We are free enough to admit that the other guy's idea gave us new insight. It is wild. We do not talk for five months and we are together for only two minutes and it seems like we are just continuing where we left the conversation at an earlier time. We both have changed radically in the time that has passed, but we are able to catch the other's pulse quickly.

Fred would come to Heinz Chapel if I asked him to. He would come with a different theological emphasis from mine. Yet, it would be important to our celebration that he would be present. The Christian is not a Christian if he is not a Jew. This is not a brotherhood rap. Fred teaches me continually that when it comes to liturgy he is where it's at. This doesn't mean that Jewish worship is the best or most meaningful the way it is done. At least, this is the judgment based on the bench marks scattered about this reflection on celebration.

I guess that I am wandering back to the history bit. Fred can draw continually upon traditions which breathe of people, suffering, and the Scriptures. When he springs a wild jazz service on his people, he has a tradition that he draws upon for guidance and support. This doesn't mean that his folk all like what he is doing. However, Jews across the country have celebrated worship in the environment that Fred and his young people have helped to create. They have made numerous tours with their original music. The service wipes you out. I was there the first night they presented it. The walls were covered with projected pictures and color patterns (four projectors). The leaders of the service were excited. They knew that they were participating in something that was new and striking and yet went back to their fathers.

Much has happened to Sim Shalom since that first celebration. It has been changed and expanded. The cast is now more polished and more sensitive in enabling the worshipers to be grasped by the entire event. They have traveled many miles to bring these kinds of experiences to worshipers across the country. One adult related how they were speeding across Colorado and took a curve on a mountain road to be confronted by an awesome view of the mountains. Without a word of direction, the whole bus of teen-agers and adults began singing Psalm 121: "I lift up my eyes to the hills. From whence does my help come? My help comes from the LORD, who made heaven and earth." This is the kind of community context from which Fred and his folk come.

It will be hard to have Fred there. I will feel the pressure of someone who has felt good liturgy. He has done good liturgy. He is an electric person who knows everything that I know. He has experienced everything that I have experienced. Yet, he is my brother and he is totally supportive. He appreciates the sense of history. The recital of holy history is imprinted upon his spirit. As God led his people out of bondage, so he does the same today. God commanded Moses to deliver a suffering people, so now he commands every Jew to release those in bondage (black, Israelite, woman, etc.). Fred provides such a good corrective to so much liturgical innovation. There must be a bedrock consisting of who and what we are as a people of God into which to anchor the free forms of liturgy. Contemporary Jews lose sight of the past as easily as other Americans. However, Judaism offers hope for Christianity in liturgy and faith. Creative spirit Duane Holm has frequently dipped back into Judaism for liturgy. He has made extensive use of the Passover celebration as a Lenten anchor for his people.

Fred loves jazz. This is really his thing. "That's my gig." I would like to be a musician. Fred and I are different. He has talent. I do not. He plays the drums. His appreciation and utilization of holy history and jazz is a fantastic combination of then and now.

The whole world of jazz could be used in our chapel celebration. Fred understands and knows this language of faith. We could do some things with the Old Testament or particularly the Psalms. He could join some of my other friends in the enjoyment of electric media as part of the celebration. I think that Fred would appreciate a style of liturgy that would reach a cross section of people.

Chuck Eaton is another friend who has combined jazz and folk music forms to reach real people. Chuck's blue-collar congregation has been carefully prepared through special celebrations to understand and enjoy the non-hymnic forms of music. Fred and Chuck would want to judge the celebration I am planning by how well it touched the lives of the gathered community.

Another thing that my representative congregation would add is interaction. This is particularly true with Fred. Just a look at his face will tell me a lot about what is and isn't happening to him in worship. This kind of transpersonal reading of what the celebration is doing within us is often lacking in worship settings. The clergyman isn't even able to tell much from just looking at bodies and faces. Yet, this kind of nonverbal communication must take place among worshipers if authentic celebration is to take place. Most of our people have been conditioned to be undemonstrative. Don't let anyone know how you really feel. Just keep it inside.

Isn't it strange that people close to you send so many messages nonverbally? When I am close to a person, I can just feel the vibes going back and forth. There is something happening between us. If you consciously break it down, you find that you notice very subtle mannerisms. Even the face takes on very different shapes under certain conditions. Marilyn tells me that my upper lip takes on a strange kind of stiffness when I am angry. Maybe this is why I now wear hair there! I still can't fool her. Fred and I seem to communicate in this way. I can just pick all kinds of attitudes and feelings from the way he moves or looks. His presence at the summer service would give a sensitive reading on where we were as a people at a given moment. The enabler of worship needs to know what is happening in order to facilitate the flow of what can yet influence what must happen.

Fred and I come from different backgrounds. What worshipers aren't from different backgrounds even with the same religious tradition? We also bear different labels. I am Christian. He is a Jew. Yet, he is my brother. I am lacking my full creative, theological essence without him. It just helps me to speculate on his presence at this community worship service. We are different and yet have the same "gig."

You are fingering my middle pages

Wow! What a trip this has been for me. So many sections of my head have been rerun through my typewriter. The simple task of putting together a chapel service for some Pittsburgh folk has been a good excuse for my getting it together about the celebration of my life.

It has been a number of working days since I left my job. My head is clearing. I am now moving a lot slower. I am smelling, tasting, and touching a lot more. Small things about my life are now becoming bigger things for me again. A few minutes ago a brother called long distance to rehearse an article he is writing for a denominational magazine. The article is on media. What he is saying is familiar. However, he is very excited about it. I am now able to get excited with him. He talks without interruption for thirty minutes. He wants my encouragement and approval. I can gladly give it. This is what creative community is really all about. However, I couldn't have done this during the last days of my overload. It is good to be back with people again!

As I look back over these meandering reflections about celebration in the electric age, I realize that it is not very linear. It really lacks the systematic polish I was trained to expect from books during my student days. It was precisely this kind of former mentality that just about destroyed me. The emotion circuitry of the electric age breaks apart when forced through channels which are too rigid. I tried to follow all the systems only to discover that the content of the input would not be so tracked. It is like getting a new job or undertaking a new task. You follow every rule or direction outlined in the manual. However, you quickly realize that this is not the way it is actually done. It is so depressing to follow the linear structures when reality just isn't designed that way.

I am now dipping back into my feelings. I am trying to rediscover my intuition and senses. These qualities have been talked about a great deal by me in the past couple of years. However, I have to move beyond talking. I have to be that which I believe and feel. There is a long way to go. These things that are so unique and fresh to me are probably obvious to others concerning the celebration of life. However, one can only be what he is at a given time.

How to recycle the ceiling and the floor

Amy is on the floor near my typing stand. She just invited me to lie on the floor beside her and look at the ceiling. My office has the ceiling covered with posters and things that friends have sent me. I had never seen it from the floor! My inclination to use the ceiling as a site for the display of art was good. However, I had not really carried the idea through to the conclusion of experiencing it from where it should be viewed! Amy forced me to enjoy the ceiling the way it should be enjoyed. It is a fantastic experience to look at the seventy-five fragments of life and faith. What a discovery! We need others in creative relationship to fully celebrate that which we already have. The faith is ours. We have it named. We have trapped it in a particular worship area at a particular time. Everything is proper and in order. However, all of this is empty form without the activity of the Holy Spirit. Again, it comes crashing home to me that the occasion of the Spirit is the community of God. There is no community without "being together in one place."

It is all there for us. What is our liturgical promise that has been fulfilled? Christ has done once and for all what we need in order to be people for others. However, this can only be known as others enable us to utilize what is given. My head keeps flashing. I can feel so many experiences from my past which seem to validate this hunch. My mind is erratic now. Little bits of experience never seem to leave. They just float around and pass by the mind's eye at the most unexpected moments.

The birthday card my parents sent to me was a very important gift. It had a brief note: "We are very proud of you and love you very much." Again, these are obvious things passed around families. Yet, this means a lot coming from two people whom I respect a great deal. I am probably still defining myself in relation to them. They have so many qualities that have been essential to my self-identity. There was a time when I felt that I couldn't compete with them. They could write and speak so much better than I could. Perhaps that is why I struck out in another direction. I remember my mother saying at one point that she made two mistakes. She sent me to school and church and I never left either one.

I have this together now. I know who I am. I can be confident in what I am becoming. It is also possible for me to appreciate and respect my parents. I can say that I love and accept them completely. This is quite a step. We are very different in our social and political points of view. Yet, we are now a family of mutual respect and love. They have always felt this way. It is just that I couldn't accept the fact that they really felt this way.

There are so many untouched areas of my mind. I am afraid to admit that I am still uptight and confused about the past, present, and future. Yet, I

It's getting better

do have a place from which to search. Life seems so fantastic. There is so much to celebrate in so many ways with so many people so many times for such a boundless faith.

Thank you for hanging in there while Dennis gets it on. The real significance of this personal reflection on worship and celebration is that I am not that much different from your people or you. I have learned in the electric environment that whenever you think of something, you should realize that others are also at the same place you are. The combination of influences is hitting other people also.

If you are not struggling with this kind of baggage, bless you. I hope that you have worked it out. However, your people are going through the same kind of sorting and identifying process. These factors are very important as you approach worship and celebration. So many books or studies on liturgy come at the quest for celebration from a given objective perspective. However, academic exercise means nothing without an exploration into the questions we have been passing around throughout this experience together. We sow in a soil. We must know that soil and know how to plant and nurture. Your people are very complex and unlimited in potentiality. Just interview a few people with a cassette tape recorder along the street. You will be amazed by the variety of the thought, the colorfulness of the language, and the concern for others. Why is it that we never have these kinds of exploratory words with people who are so important to us? We don't take into our arms those who are lonely; we don't hold the hands of those who are filled with sorrow; we don't rejoice with those who just made it big. We don't share these kinds of things with our brothers and sisters. These are not strangers who come to celebration. They come because of what God has done with us in Jesus Christ. Everything in their heads is our responsibility. We care because God first cared for us. All that old theological-biblical language means something if we commune with our brothers and sisters.

Neighbors

During the past few days I have taken the time to get into my neighbors' things. I have often been quite glib about how hip I was and how uptight they are. I find that we are both uptight. There are some fantastic people around here. It takes time to celebrate the wholeness of life. Maybe our church celebrations should be two or three hours long! Maybe we should do the whole Christian life in a microcosm experience together (fellowship, worship, study, and performing miracles). It takes time to have time.

I am learning about myself and other people all over again. This is not all of my back pages (past) nor my front pages (future). I guess that I am now sharing my middle pages. I am going to learn more about celebration by celebrating with my folks. It is good—very good.

You know what they do in the desert when they got no water?

So many of the ideas about liturgy as celebration discussed by those doing contemporary worship are familiar. As I have suggested, just about every form of religious worship has been tried by somebody at some time. These forms have been tried for different reasons and have had different meanings. However, when you come back to the local setting you suspect that the forms of the past are never going to change. There is a resilience built into most existent liturgies. I guess that the function of faith recital is to preserve that which is familiar. The people must have well-worn footholds to keep their footing as they scramble for the heights of celebration. Yet, there is also the possibility that well-worn paths may lead to a place no longer important.

It is so frustrating to be in a local setting and meet with a strange bundle of attitudes. On the one hand, most people agree with the reasons behind creative or meaningful probes for liturgy. They can give lip service to the importance of Communion or the Mass being the opportunity for the people of God to confront the promises of God and each other. The local worship committee can strongly affirm the fact that we must come to such

What happens to the thanksgiving dimension to the Lord's Supper?

Scotland

a sacrament with the total surrender of self. Yet, the instructions to laymen assisting in the service include: "May we suggest conservative dress for this occasion." What does conformity of dress have to do with the immediacy and honesty of worship?

The status quo of religious celebration in local settings can be painful for those who now feel and see something other than what they can actually experience. Even our words about the meaning and power of liturgy have not been translated into the forms we use. The worshiper is often caught in a living lie. What his lips are saying as he reads a prayer in unison is denied by his feelings and experiences. The clergyman says words of hope and love while the people cannot experience them because of the forms which restrict such experiences. The traditional systems of liturgy often stress factors which have nothing to do with the essences of the message. We worry about clothes for liturgy and not the hearts of believers.

Marilyn and I were guests of Gillian Carter at the retreat center located in Dunblane, Scotland. It is a fantastic blend of the past with the needs of the 70's and 80's. Folks gather in the restored row houses for quiet. theological exploration and renewal. They seek a theological posture for their working lives. During the weekend of our visit a local mental institution was giving inmates a "holiday" at Dunblane. The chapel at the facility is built in the cellar of an ancient house which once stood in the town during pre-Christian times. The service which the mental patients and we attended was quite simple. The Bible was read, words were spoken, hymns were sung, and prayers were said. One middle-aged lady held a doll throughout the service. She rocked it gently and sung a lullaby. A person next to her turned and harshly told her to be quiet. She repeated the admonition several times. The lady with the doll stopped rocking it. She stared out in space for a few minutes. She then started to whisper to the people around, "Shh. Shh. Be quiet!" This was her role throughout the rest of the service. She had picked up the stressed factor of silence as being the thrust of the service. We had told her to be quiet and she was going to make her contribution to worship in this important way.

This kind of distortion is what we experience in all of life. We accept the structures, the things people shout the loudest about, and we are not able to dip into the essence which gave these reflections form. How do we start again and yet bring the past with us as a well from which we can draw nourishment for today and tomorrow?

Tom was a friend when it counted. He was a black construction worker. He had been around for a long time. This powerhouse of a man was an excellent mason and carpenter. Of course, he received the wages of a laborer because black people didn't belong to the trade unions in that city. I could understand how resentful he might be toward white college kids like me. We whipped into his wage bracket for a summer and then moved out for a great future. He remained there with no future. Tom was a together dude. He liked the college kids if they held their own. We made it together because I jumped into the clay pit and worked like hell to prove myself. I may have been working hard for the wrong reasons. However, it was he who told me to take it easy or I would kill myself. He passed me the sacramental cup of coffee which proclaimed acceptance and love. I remember one day when I thought I wasn't going to make it. It was hot and humid. We were forced to dig in the sun without any shade. The heat was getting to me. I asked for water. Tom said that the man with the water wouldn't be around for another thirty minutes. I complained that I didn't think that I would make it. He smiled. "You know what they do in the desert when they got no water?" He paused a devilishly long time. "They go without!"

Many people are now going without. It isn't because there isn't any source of nourishment. We simply don't know how to get to it. Even when we do find the cache of power, we don't know how to deliver it. Where do we find the right vessels? It is obvious from this journey of probing we have taken together that the context in which I find my answers to these questions and others is the community of brothers and sisters. These folk have different shapes, labels, and life-styles. However, they are there to aid me in the quest for celebration.

You should know some of these folk who celebrate life:

Mose Henry—brother-performer-song writer.

Jay Balas—multimedia liturgy freak.

Roy Lloyd—musician, Simon-Garfunkel liturgist.

Russell Block—creative liturgy enabler of every medium.

Digging and sweating in the summer

Some of the Folk

Phineas Washer—hunger liturgist and prober.

Fredric S. Pomerantz—brother and creative jazz-multimedia liturgist.

David Leachman—multimedia celebrant.

Jane Mall—sister—creative teacher and celebrant with every medium.

Roger Ortmayer—creative enabler with music, sound, sight, and touch from the beginning of creative liturgy.

John and Mary Harrell—creative brother and sister who enable others to celebrate all of life.

Al Johnson—thoughtfully creative ecumenical liturgist.

Jacinta Van Winckel—loving sister who enables others to discover the source of worship.

Roger Boekenhauer—creative brother who searches the liturgical meaning of color and symbols.

Kent Schneider—creative musician, liturgy enabler, and worship community leader.

Paul Keller—Kairos enabler of films, drama, etc.

Duane Holm—brother who makes the bread rise in all kinds of liturgical settings.

Larry L. Thornton—member of creative team which enabled "The Church at Worship in an Urban Age" ($1.00) to be written and shared.

Lewis A. Briner—creative teacher of liturgy who prepared the extensive "Annotated Bibliography of Recent Resources for Liturgical Renewal" and shared lots of insight with many people.

Doris Schwerin—creative sister who celebrates with language and feeling.

William F. Hamel, Sr.—creative sharer of liturgical probes.

Stan Summers—creative brother who unleashes others through celebration of film and art.

Myron Slater—creative biblical translator and pop liturgist who shares so much.

Robert L. Short—creative brother who helps us celebrate the Peanuts of liturgy.

Ted Siverns—brother who cooly uses everything to celebrate the Good News.

Ken Dobson—creative brother who is able to recycle more items for celebration than anyone I know.

Chuck Eaton—brother who makes celebration out of music and life.

Jack Ridl—celebrating brother who writes, sings, and enables others to worship.

Steve Brezzo—creative puppeteer and celebrant of life through art.

David A. Elliott, III—creative liturgical enabler who dips into The Who, The Beatles, etc., to celebrate.

Jan and Ed Jepson—innovative liturgists who explore the world of penance and forgiveness through various media.

Vern Hockenberry—sensitive electric liturgist who enables worshipers to feel and respond to the Good News.

Frank Ramsey; William Pennock, Jr.; Bob Mayo; James Davis—creative brothers who assisted in the development of Electric Liturgy's sound skin.

Toni, Antonia, Samuel, Jill, Amy—folk AT THE GARAGE.

There are more folk who have loved and supported me even when I was more strung out than I am now. They have been patient and understanding even when I failed to fill in all the holes in my mind and thoughts. Some folk will help me at the summer celebration because they have supported me apart from this particular manifestation of my ministry. David H. Barnes helps to give order and meaning to the things I write. He has been super critic on syntax, grammar, and all that jazz. He is my brother and comrade. Betsey McClure has done a fantastic job of getting the typescript in shape in a matter of days. Her ability to help get this thing into print has been most important.

Marilyn, Amy, and Jill are the love of my life. They make celebration possible. It is their love which has nurtured my creativity. I have come home from my overloaded life to be with them. It is good being home— very good, indeed.

I am going to stir around all these thoughts and ideas shared by so many people and come up with something for the Heinz Chapel event. I am convinced now that I must do it as part of a community. I think that I will call upon Jack Ridl and other friends. Perhaps we can find some particular

Love Notes

structure as a community of friends sharing what we have to celebrate with others. I think that celebration is something never complete. It is an agonizing process of living, loving, and believing which flows with possibility. The God of this faith doesn't leave us to ''go without.'' It is there if we just take it. I am going to try. I hope that you are, brothers and sisters. It is possible to celebrate even in the electric age—with a lot of help from your friends.